Participatory Workshops

For Carolyn Jones

Participatory Workshops

A Sourcebook of 21 Sets of Ideas and Activities

Robert Chambers

Earthscan Publications Ltd
London • Sterling, VA

First published in the UK and USA in 2002 by
Earthscan Publications Ltd

Copyright © Robert Chambers, 2002

A catalogue record for this book is available from the British Library

ISBN: 1 85383 863 2 paperback
        1 85383 862 4 hardback

Typesetting by PCS Mapping & DTP, Newcastle upon Tyne
Printed and bound by Creative Print and Design (Wales), Ebbw Vale
Cover design by Yvonne Booth
Illustrations by Regina Faul-Doyle

For a full list of publications please contact:

Earthscan Publications Ltd
120 Pentonville Road
London, N1 9JN, UK
Tel: +44 (0)20 7278 0433
Fax: +44 (0)20 7278 1142
Email: earthinfo@earthscan.co.uk
http://www.earthscan.co.uk

22883 Quicksilver Drive, Sterling, VA 20166–2012, USA

Earthscan is an editorially independent subsidiary of Kogan Page Ltd and publishes in
association with WWF-UK and the International Institute for Environment and
Development

This book is printed on elemental chlorine-free paper

Contents

PART 5 ANALYSIS AND LEARNING

PART 6 BEHAVIOUR AND AWARENESS

CONTENTS

Acknowledgements

Collecting and writing these 21s has been fun, a hobby over almost ten years. It has also been a long process, and I am grateful to colleagues and funders for their patience and support. All members of the Participation Group at the Institute of Development Studies at the University of Sussex have contributed and helped. Earlier funding from Danida, the Ford Foundation, NOVIB, the Overseas Development Administration, the Paul Hamlyn Foundation, SAREC, SDC (the Swiss Agency for Development and Cooperation) and Sida (the Swedish International Development Agency), and more recent support to the Participation Group from DFID (the UK Department for International Development), Sida and SDC have made space and given freedom to work on this.

I have been extraordinarily fortunate to have had opportunities to try to facilitate and help with training (and to be tolerated when muddling and messing up) in different contexts and with different people. There is no way I could ever recognize all those I have learnt from and with. To those inadvertently left out of these acknowledgements I apologize. To all, named and unnamed, I am grateful. Those with whom I have been a co-facilitator or trainer, or from whose facilitation, training or related advice I have learnt over the past 20 years include:

Binoy Acharya, G B Adhikari, Selina Adjebeng-Asem, Eloy Anello, David Archer, Heidi Attwood, Anindo Banerjee, Kiran Bhatia, Jutta Blauert, Matthias zur Bonsen, Karen Brock, Fiona Chambers, Jenny Chambers, Francis Chirunga, Gordon Conway, David Cooperrider, Andrea Cornwall, Francoise Coupal, Tessa Cousins, Rosalind David, John Devavaram, Tony Dogbe, Rashida Dohad, P Durgaprasad, Rosalind Eyben, Aloysius Fernandes, Nicola Foroni, Reiner Forster, Sheelu Francis, Keshav Gautam, John Gaventa, Gerry Gill, Jonathan Goodhand, Elizabeth Gould, Irene Guijt, Rachel Hinton, Irungu Houghton, Enamul Huda, Ravi Jayakaran, Carolyn Jones, John Jones, Vicky Johnson, Sam Joseph, Dee Jupp, Amar Jyoti, Jacqueline Kabambe, Barbara Kaim, Monsiapile Kajimbwa, Kamal Kar, Kausar Khan, Prem Kumar, Somesh Kumar, Hanna Laitinen, Josh Levene, Nguyen Thi Phuong Mai, Saiti Makuku, Humera Malik, Antonella Mancini, Alan Margolis, Stella Maranga, Mwajuma Masaiganah, Jimmy Mascarenhas, Ophelia Mascarenhas, Yaduvendra Mathur, Simon Maxwell, Rosemary McGee, Grace Mukasa, Neela Mukherjee, Sammy Musyoki, Deepa Narayan, Rose Nierras, Kate Norrish, Elkanah Odembo, Rasha Omar, Charles Owusu, Sachin Oza, Gopa Pandey, Bardolf Paul, Ditdit Pelegrina, Patti Petesch, Jethro Pettit, Bimal Phnuyal, Kamal Phuyal, Michel Pimbert, Garett Pratt, Jules Pretty, Timothy Pyrch, Vidya Ramachandran, Sitapathi Rao, Roger Ricafort, Jennifer Rietbergen-McCracken, Eva Robinson, Dorothea Rojahn, Mallika Samaranayake, Stephen Sandford, Ian Scoones, Patta Scott-Villiers, Rachel Searle-Mbullu, Tilly Sellers, Anil C Shah, Meera Kaul Shah, Parmesh Shah, E M Shashidharan, Anton Simanovitz, Kamal Singh,

Ramesh Singh, Christian Sorrenson, Jane Stevens, John Thompson, Koy Thomson, Hermann (Timmy) Tillmann, Thelma Trench, Karen Twining, Mary Underwood, Khemraj Upadhyaya, Meenu Vadera, Timo Voipio, Alice Welbourn, and Valli Yanni.

Without the above, there is no way this sourcebook could have been compiled. At the same time, responsibility for errors, omissions or defects is mine and mine alone.

In a long process like this, encouragement is more important than many realize. This I have had at intervals from many colleagues, especially Glenis Morison whose enthusiasm lifted me at a time of low morale.

Much is owed to Regina Faul-Doyle for the skill, creativity and humour of her illustrations, distracting attention so effectively from deficiencies in the text. Thanks are due to the Sustainable Agriculture Group at the International Institute for Environment and Development for permission to reproduce four of her drawings from *A Trainer's Guide for Participatory Learning and Action* [see **21**:1].

At Earthscan, I have appreciated the enthusiasm and support of Jonathan Sinclair Wilson and the detailed corrections and suggestions made by Akan Leander and the copy editor Gillian Bourn. To the members of the Participation Group at IDS I am grateful for their unfailing support and for their tolerant indulgence as we passed the 21st, and then 22nd and 23rd announcements that the end was in sight. I have a special debt to Jethro Pettit who gave freely of his expertise, wise advice, encouragement and energy, co-authored the section on materials, and read and commented on the entire text, making many good suggestions and restoring my confidence.

Finally, I thank Jane Stevens. Her contributions have been beyond measure. Again and again, her professional advice has been spot on. With unfailing good humour and support in not 21 but 2100 ways she has been a tower of strength. It has been a privilege and pleasure to work together on this. Without her efforts and good judgement this book would have had many, many more defects; and without her encouragement and commitment, it would never have been finished.

Robert Chambers
February 2002

ACKNOWLEDGEMENTS

Glossary of Terms and Meanings

Brainstorm	An intensive open-ended interaction to generate ideas or solve problems.
Buzz	A quick discussion in small groups, often twos or threes.
Energizer	An activity that wakes us up and helps us to be more alert and active.
Facipulate	Facilitate in a manipulative manner.
Facilitators	Used to embrace all, whether they are called facilitators, trainers, faculty, lecturers or teachers, who facilitate, train, teach or co-learn, whether this is through workshops, training courses or classes.
Flow diagram	A graphical presentation of a sequence of events [see **21**:4, p3.49].
Ground sorting	Refers to sorting collections of cards on the ground. This is usually more participatory than doing it on a wall or even on a table.
IDS	Institute of Development Studies at the University of Sussex, Brighton BN1 9RE, UK.
IIED	The International Institute for Environment and Development, 3 Endsleigh Street, London WC1H ODD.
INGO	International non-governmental organization.
Lowers	People who in a given context are inferior or subordinate to *uppers*. A person can be a lower in one context and an upper in another.
Mapping	Refers to maps and spatial diagrams made by participants. Common forms are social, resource and mobility maps showing, respectively, people, resources, and where people go for services and other purposes [see **21**:4, pp3.24, 3.26 and 3.35].
Matrix scoring	A visual method of analysis in which items are compared according to a number of criteria. The items are usually listed across the top and the criteria down the side, and a matrix or grid drawn. The boxes are then scored, each item according to each criterion, often using beans, stones or other counters [see **21**:4, p3.38].
NGO	Non-governmental organization.
North	Refers to what are variously also known as developed, industrialized and OECD countries, formerly described as the First World.
Participants	Includes all who take part in workshops, training courses and classes, whether as colleagues, co-learners, clients, members or students.
Plenary	A meeting of all participants in a workshop, course or class.

PRA/PLA Participatory Rural Appraisal/Participatory Learning and Action. PRA is increasingly taken as Participatory Reflection and Action [see **3**].

Role play An activity in which the behaviour of others is acted out in an imaginary situation.

South Refers to what are variously known as developing or non-industrialized countries, formerly described as the Third World.

Spider diagram A diagram like a spider's web. The 'spokes' or radii of the web represent dimensions or criteria, scores on which are joined up [see **7**:6].

Time line A listing of events in sequence, often with approximate dates.

Trend or change diagram One of many forms of diagram showing changes or trends [see **21**:4, diagram, p3.55].

Uppers People who in a given context are dominant or superior to *lowers*. A person can be an upper in one context and a lower in another.

Venn Venn diagramming is a PRA tool in which objects of different sizes, shapes or colours (often circular pieces of paper or stones) are arranged to show relative importance and relationships of organizations, individuals, services etc. Also known as chapati (South Asia), tortilla (Latin America) and dumpling (West Indies) diagramming [see **21**:4, p3.36].

VIPP Visualisation in Participatory Programmes [see **21**:14].

Wimbledon syndrome Named after the annual international tennis tournament at Wimbledon in the UK, referring to looking rapidly and repeatedly left and right as in watching tennis, or for the middle person in a discussion sitting in a line.

You are the facilitator, convenor, trainer or teacher for whom this book is primarily written. In an empowering and participatory spirit, 'you' can also be one or more of 'them'. Many of the activities can be facilitated by participants. Handing over to them introduces variety, a new dynamic and quite often innovation; it gives you a chance to learn from how they do it (so often differently and better than you would have); and it gives you space to relax and prepare for what comes next.

Important exception: You, in this sense, should in no circumstances read the 20th 21: 21 Tips for Surviving Workshops. In that section 'you' refers exclusively to those who are seriously shy and have a horror of participation. It was written for them and them only. The degree of moral hazard to which you would expose yourself were you to ignore this injunction defies description.

ZOPP Ziel-Orientierte Projekt Planung, a form of logical framework for planning.

On this Sourcebook

This book is for all who try to help others learn and change. The ideas, activities and tips are for facilitators, trainers and teachers, and for those who organize and manage workshops, training and courses. There is something here for participatory teachers and trainers; for organizers, moderators and facilitators who want their conferences and workshops to be interactive; for staff in training institutions who want to enliven their courses; for faculty and teachers in universities, colleges and schools who would like to enable students to do more of their own analysis, helping each other learn; and for those engaged in management training who want to widen their repertoire.

Not everything is covered. This is not directly about how to be a good facilitator: that is well covered in 21 Sources of Ideas for Trainers and Facilitators at the end of this sourcebook. Nor is everything in some sense 'new'; there are a few worthy old chestnuts. But I hope users will find ideas that intrigue and provoke them into trying out something they have not done before. I may have missed something, but I have yet to find anything elsewhere quite as full on as, say, seating arrangements, ways of forming groups, handling large workshops, or even tips and options for analysis and feedback. To any reader who can point me to sources that cover these more fully I shall indeed be grateful (email: participation@ids.ac.uk).

This is a collection, a menu à la carte, a source, not a summation. Nor is it all heavy stuff. An earlier title was *Serious Fun with 21*, referring to the 21 sets of 21 items. It originates in participatory workshops and training in which I have been involved, and in attempts to move from 'teaching' to participatory learning. These are activities that seek to make learning quicker, deeper, more enduring and more fun.

I have used most of the exercises myself. I have included a few that I have not used because they look good and I have been told they are good. I have avoided approaches that go deep into personal emotions. For those, one needs special training and temperament. I find some personal change approaches intrusive, and prefer to keep things lighter, with laughter as a lightning conductor to discharge embarrassment rather than a flood of tears to express distress. Programmes and workshops for profound personal change can surely be immensely valuable, but as a specimen of the species 'middle-class Englishman' I cannot help being who and what I am. I value some privacy and try to uphold the basic human right not to be evangelized or got at. At the same time, this sourcebook is full of advice and injunctions that I fail to follow myself, enabling me to be patriotic in maintaining English national standards of hypocrisy.

I have tried to make this sourcebook easy to use. The table of contents gives an idea of what there is and where to look. The introductions of all except the shortest

MENU À LA CARTE

sections have a list of their 21 entries. At the back of the book the entries are listed and indexed in alphabetical order. Cross-references in the text use two numbers: for example, **7**:18 refers to entry 18 in section 7. Each of the 21s is meant to stand on its own. This is also my rationalization for why a few points are made in more than one place.

Finally, to confess. I am not a professional teacher, trainer or facilitator. But I do love ideas and experiences of different ways of doing things. So, this is an amateur's collection. It has been fun putting it together. I hope it will be accessible to amateurs and professionals alike; and that, as these 21s are tried out and improved upon, all – whether trainers, facilitators, teachers, course or workshop convenors, participants or students – will learn, gain something and enjoy.

ON THIS SOURCEBOOK

Introduction

My effrontery in putting together this collection demands explanation. I have never had a day's teacher training. Early in my 'career', in Kenya, I was a pretty hopeless administrator and manager. For those in administrative services around the world who are incompetent, there are four main trajectories: out of the service; exile to a remote posting where harm done will be less noticed; into an evaluation unit; or transfer to train others. In those days, out of the service was properly imminent for all foreign administrators but had not come quickly enough to get me out of the way; I had already done a spell in a remote posting where the damage I did, although serious, was localized (I have been back to apologize); and evaluation had not been invented. So, I was consigned to be a trainer in the new Kenya Institute of Administration. To George Bernard Shaw's 'He who can, does. He who cannot, teaches' can be added 'He who cannot teach, administers', and finally, 'He who cannot administer, teaches administrators'. (The male-biased syntax is historically and perhaps also empirically correct.)

The experience, though, was wonderful. It was brilliantly challenging and enjoyable. With fellow amateur trainers I was forced to improvise and invent wildly on the run. I conducted (the word used in those days) three six-month courses almost end to end for new administrators. 'Learning by doing' meant a multitude of mistakes, and trying not to fall off a vertiginous learning curve.

Five lessons stand out from that full and frantic time and from subsequent experience:

The first was to *ration nervous energy*. At first, I was terribly tense and uptight before sessions. But you cannot survive with stratospheric levels of anxiety. The more facilitating, training or teaching you do in a period, and the closer together the occasions are, the less time there is for worry. Nervous energy rations itself.

Some adrenalin is good, though. If, before a workshop or session, you shake and shiver, drum your fingers and bite your nails, and the butterflies flutter in the pit of your stomach, take comfort. It is better to be too nervous than not nervous enough. The thing is to get the level right. If you start too nervously you can work on becoming less so. Unless you pack up completely this will happen naturally with time and experience. But if you start complacently and confidently, it may be harder to get anxious enough to give of your best. Better to tremble with trepidation than to be one of Robert Browning's 'finished and finite clods, untroubled by a spark'.

The second lesson was to *cultivate stamina*. This I have found has a lot to do with fitness and relaxation. Up to the time of writing I have been lucky to be able to jog in the early mornings before workshops, training or 'teaching'. This has a treble function. It keeps you fit; it keeps safe a private time for yourself on your own, free from the social effort of participation, a time when your mind can wander and ideas come (and go); and it shows you the world around you (often intensely interesting in new environments). Some meditate. Some do yoga. Some go for aerobics. Some pray. Some perform extended rituals of washing, hawking, spitting, brushing teeth and other aspects of toilet. Whatever it is that one does, the knowledge that there will be this sacred time on one's own each day, and the sense of physical wellbeing that comes with exercise (and/or washing and the rest) – these contribute to the stamina of being able to keep going day after long day.

CULTIVATE STAMINA

The third lesson was to *hand over the stick*. When I started as a trainer I hadn't a clue about this. I thought every buck stopped with me. I had to do everything, fill every gap, answer every question, plan every event, deal with every personal problem. That was stressful, to say the least. It has taken me, dare I say it, 40 years to make some progress towards recognizing that other people can usually do things better than I can; that in any group of people there is a wealth of relevant experience and analytical capability; that others can suggest answers to many of the most difficult questions; that responsibilities can be divided up and shared. In short, that participatory approaches – handing over the stick – reduce stress and enhance effectiveness.

The fourth was to *be optimally unprepared*. This is a paradox of participation. Participatory processes cannot be 'properly planned', where 'properly' refers to fixed content and strict timetables. I have seen training schedules, especially from francophone West Africa, with timings down to the minute. I doubt the value of such precision. Whatever the rhetoric, it fits and fosters top-down teaching. If you have planned a session in exact detail, you will be thrown off by participation: 'I am sorry, we have no time for that.' Of course some planning is good. Of course some things have to be covered. Of course time management matters. But you cannot fit exploring, experiencing and learning to tight, preset timetables. When everyone is gripped, participatory appraisal training can go on to midnight and beyond. Knocking off at 5 o'clock would be, if not a death blow, at least a disabling amputation. At the same time, no one could have said, 'Today we are going to go on until after midnight'; there would have been groans of disbelief. Good participatory processes are predictably unpredictable.

Part of the key is to know what has to be planned and what is better left open. Good logistics are basic – the fundamentals of workshop space, equipment and materials, and of board, accommodation, finance and allowances. Transport schedules, room bookings and arrangements to meet people in communities may need to be efficient, timely and held to. But where possible, flexibility should be built in – for travel, for meals, for times of return from fieldwork, for parts of a programme.

Optimal unpreparedness liberates a facilitator (to mix the metaphors) to go with the flow, roll with the punches, and steer by sailing and tacking with the wind. Good workshops are more like a sea voyage than putting up a building. There is less a syllabus to tick off, and more a direction to travel in and a process to experience.

INTRODUCTION

The fifth lesson, supporting all the others, was to *develop a repertoire*. In part this was a stock of things to do. It is easier to be optimally unprepared if you are confident that you have lots you can draw on without further preparation. It also helps to have activities prepared *in case*, ready for use as options if they make sense. I hope that the stock of these 21s will help here. There is much more, though, to a repertoire than just a stock. It took me time to realize that it is also being able and willing, often interactively, to find new things to do and new ways to do them. It was when more participatory training came along, for me in the late 1980s, that I began to see how much more versatile others were who had the courage and confidence to innovate. The participatory approach to training opened up a new dimension. It was like moving from 2D space into 3D. The new dimension was improvising and inventing. The shifts from lecturing to facilitating, and from teaching to learning with others and helping others to learn, opened up new behaviours and new interactions. The space for experiment and innovation soon seemed unbounded. The field experience of participatory approaches, methods and behaviours in South Asia and elsewhere, played its part in this. If outsiders were to facilitate local people's own appraisal, analysis, planning, action, monitoring and evaluation, the training of those outsiders had to be in the same participatory mode; not teaching but enabling others to experience and learn for themselves.

In the late 1980s and early 1990s, there was an exhilarating (it seemed almost magical) explosion of participatory training associated with PRA (originally Participatory Rural Appraisal but now increasingly either Participatory Reflection and Action or Participatory Learning and Action – PLA).[1] Much had gone before and contributed ideas, experiences and inspiration: *Training for Transformation* (Hope and Timmel, 1984), NGOs' training, psychotherapeutic group techniques, manuals for teaching, training and learning [see **21**], and management training, especially the work of Alan Margolis. Some approaches, techniques and exercises also seemed new, generated by new challenges, needs and opportunities. Those who pioneered included the Sustainable Agriculture Programme at the International Institute for Environment and Development (IIED) in London, and many PRA trainers in Asia, Africa and elsewhere. In full measure there was excitement and fun. And much exchange, innovation and learning took place when trainers worked together. So the shared stock of things to do grew and grew. And in 1995 much that had been learnt was brought together by IIED in *Participatory Learning and Action: A Trainer's Guide* (Pretty et al, 1995) which remains a splendid source of good advice and excellent exercises [see **21**:1].

So why now these 21 21s?

Let us start with what they are not. The numbers have nothing to do with the millennium and the 21st century. So:

---

1 For further information see *RRA Notes*, later *PLA Notes*, published three times a year by the International Institute for Environment and Development, 3 Endsleigh Street, London WC1H ODD, and available free to subscribers in developing countries. See also www.ids.ac.uk/ids/particip for details of the sources and materials available.

INTRODUCTION

Neither more nor less, why do they run
each of them to the same 'twenty-one'?
    One reason's obscure
    And not very pure
But the main one's quite simple – it's fun!

The obscure and not very pure reason goes back to family history and my child-hood. As children, the only gambling game my sister and I were allowed to play with our parents was pontoon (in French, 'vingt-et-un') in which a hand adding up to 21 is a winner. Also, my sister and I were promised, continuing a family tradition, £21 each on our 21st birthdays if by then we had neither smoked tobacco nor drunk alcohol. With inflation the financial incentive became derisory, and changing mores eroded any inclination to abstinence. But by then the number was embed-ded. So when I challenged myself to list different ways of forming groups, 21 was the number that came to mind. 21 tips for workshops with large numbers followed. And then the lamentable idea of compiling 21 21s became a compulsive recreation.

In the meantime I found myself in the mid- and late 1990s no longer engaged in any pretence of honest field research, but more and more facilitating and taking part in workshops, training and teaching. These activities then became my field-work; and my research became participant observation in action research – collecting, testing, adapting, improvising and inventing approaches, sequences, exercises and ways of doing things. To work on the 21s added point and pleasure to life and forced me to search to fill the lists. It made every workshop, training and conference I went to an intriguing study of methodology and process, a potential source of experience and ideas. So these 21 21s began as fun, and fun remains a thread throughout.

They are also collected from many sources. I have tried to acknowledge those I know, but many of the origins are lost in the mists of time. To those who are not recognized, I apologize. If you are one, let me hope you can find it some consola-tion that this sourcebook will carry your contribution to more people.

In the spirit of participatory sharing, anything in this collection can be photo-copied or translated. If reproduction is for commercial use, permission will need to be obtained from the publisher, and if you want to translate the whole book, whether or not for commercial use I shall be delighted, but please contact me or the publisher first. We should be able to tell you whether translations already exist. All of which expresses the fond and vain delusions of an author who dares to imagine that anyone might want to translate any of this sourcebook in the first place.

Anyway, whoever you are, if you can, enjoy. Do better than I have. Make up your own 21s. And please, share them around.

Robert Chambers
August 2001

INTRODUCTION

Part 1
Brief Basics

1

21 Dos

If you are repeating what you did two years ago, is something wrong?

When in doubt,

- **do something new. Be of good heart.**
- **Fail forwards.**
- **Bounce back.**
- **Celebrate learning.**

and

- **experiment**
- **innovate**
- **invent**
- **improvise**
- **dare**
- **risk**
- **seek**
- **explore**
- **discover**
- **collect**

- **adapt**
- **combine**
- **vary**
- **sequence**
- **reflect**
- **self-critique**
- **change**
- **share**
- **spread**
- **enjoy**

and

- **make your own list**

2

21 Questions when Preparing for Participatory Workshops and Learning

A SKELETON CHECKLIST

1 Why?

What is the purpose? Who determines it? What experience, sharing, analysis, learning or other end is sought?

2 How does it fit?

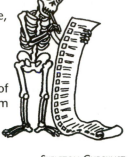

How does the workshop fit into longer-term processes of learning and change? If there are no such longer-term processes, should you undertake it at all? Or should you negotiate with the sponsors for commitment to make it fit?

SKELETON CHECKLIST

3 Who and how many?

Who will the people be? How should they be selected, and against what criteria? How many should there or will there be?

4 What expectations?

What will they expect? How can you find out?

5 How participatory?

What sort of process? How participatory can and should it be? How much can participants do themselves?

6 What is your part?

What is your role and contribution? Trainer, facilitator, co-learner...?

7 Who else?

Who else could, should or will help, take part or co-facilitate?

8 Where?

What venue should be sought, against what criteria?

9 When?

When should it be? How long should it take? What should the timetable be for preparations?

10 Finance

What will it cost and how will it be paid for? What allowances, if any, will participants expect and receive, and who will pay for these?

11 Programme

With whom, where, when and how should the programme be planned? Who should be consulted?

12 Languages

What languages will be used? Who may be marginalized by language? What can be done about it? Are interpreters needed?

13 Logistics

Who – not a facilitator and not a participant – will handle travel and logistics? Are extra support staff needed?

14 Materials and equipment

What will be needed – materials, equipment, transport?

15 Participants' preparation

What should be sent to participants in advance? What should they do in advance?

16 Local liaison

Do arrangements need to be made with a local administration, local communities or other organizations? Who should make these?

17 Outputs

What outputs will there be? A written record? A report? A video? Notes? If so, who will be responsible and what will be the later value, circulation and use of the output(s)?

18 Follow-up

What follow-up can and should there be? With participants? With their organizations? Locally, with administration, communities and organizations?

19 Your preparation

What do you need to do to prepare? When and how can you do this? What help do you need?

20 Flexibility

What is best left unplanned?

21 What is missing from this list?

What else should you be thinking about and preparing for?

3

21 PRA/PLA Behaviours[1]

PRA originated in East Africa and India as Participatory Rural Appraisal. It has been described as a family of approaches, behaviours and methods for enabling people to do their own appraisal, analysis and planning, take their own action, and do their own monitoring and evaluation. It often involves people in groups developing their own visuals such as diagrams and maps, drawing on the ground with sticks or on paper with pens, and using counters like beans, seeds or stones. Following the lead of Pakistan, the letters PRA have increasingly been taken to stand for Participatory Reflection and Action. Other practitioners describe what they do as Participatory Learning and Action (PLA) to stress inclusive methodological pluralism. PRA/PLA has spread to many countries and from South to North, with applications in many domains.

PEOPLE IN GROUPS

This is one person's list of behaviours for PRA/PLA. They are derived from fieldwork and apply also to participatory workshops, training and helping one another to learn.

Why not make out your own list of dos and don'ts before you read mine?

None of these behaviours is an absolute. There are occasions for doing the don'ts and not doing the dos. The point is to ask whether we do the don'ts too much and don't do the dos enough. Good facilitation and empowering others demands action, reflection, learning and change, which are continuous and have no end. No one ever arrives. The moment any of us thinks we've arrived, we're lost. These are working hypotheses for constant questioning and modification.
There are a few Don'ts

---

1 Visit www.ids.ac.uk/ids/particip for abstracts of many sources on PRA and PLA and how to obtain them, and for contacts in different countries. For a discussion of PRA and PLA by Jim Rugh and a guide to methods by Meera Kaul Shah see *Embracing Participation in Development: Wisdom from the Field* [see **21**:4].

DON'T

- rush
- lecture
- criticize
- interrupt
- dominate
- sabotage
- take yourself too seriously

Much is positive with 21 Dos

Do

- Use your own best judgement at all times
- Introduce yourself, establish rapport
- Respect, be nice to people
- 'Ask them'[2]
- Facilitate
- Empower and support, be confident that 'They can do it'[3]
- Hand over the stick[4]
- Be sensitive
- Share
- Watch, listen, learn
- Embrace error, learn from mistakes
- Relax
- Unlearn, abandon preconceptions
- Be self-aware and self-critical
- Triangulate[5]
- Seek optimal ignorance[6]
- Be honest
- Improvise
- Be optimally unprepared and flexible
- Have fun, joke, enjoy
- Innovate and invent – try new things, be bold, take risks

---

2 'Ask them' refers to those who are 'upper' asking those who are 'lower', questions that reverse the upper–lower (eg teacher–student) relationship, such as 'what is your view?', 'how would you think of doing this?', or 'how did I behave?'

3 'They can do it' means that uppers assume that lowers can do something until it is proved otherwise. Usually lowers can do more than uppers suppose or than they realize themselves. A condition for discovering lowers' abilities is that uppers have confidence in them.

4 'Hand over the stick' has literal and metaphorical meanings. Literally, it means handing over a stick, baton, pointer, pen, chalk or other symbol of authority or means of expression. Metaphorically it means transferring authority and initiative.

5 'Triangulate' means seek multiple perspectives to cross-check, qualify and correct.

6 'Optimal ignorance' means not finding out more than needs to be found out, or not measuring with more precision than is necessary.

This list draws on several sources. One is Chapters 6 and 7 of *Whose Reality Counts?* (Chambers, 1997, pp102–87). Another is papers compiled and edited by Tilly Sellers as part of the Young People and Sexual Health Project, Department of Public Health Medicine, University of Hull, December 1995. That has an excellent shorter list:

'Facilitators should

show respect

establish rapport

abandon preconceptions

hand over the stick

watch, listen, learn

learn from mistakes

be self-critical and self-aware

be flexible

support and share

be honest'

HAND OVER THE STICK

4

21 PRA/PLA Questions to Ask Oneself

I wrote this section with facilitating PRA/PLA fieldwork in mind. It can also apply to workshops, courses, training and teaching.

Self-critical awareness is one of the principles of PRA. In the mode of 'use your own best judgement at all times', each of us can list our own questions for self-examination. I have enjoyed dreaming up my list. You could enjoy making your own, and it should serve you better than mine. In the spirit of pluralism, let diversity rule.

If you agree, go ahead, do it, and do not read on.

If you disagree, or for whatever perverse reason do read on, please treat these questions lightly. And do better yourself.

The danger with any list is stopping or delaying action. I like the saying 'start, stumble, self-correct, share'. Or the business executive's motto 'Ready, fire, aim'. We learn most by doing, by committing to action, by making and recognizing mistakes, by gaining experience the hard way. We learn little by tying ourselves into knots with critical introspection before daring to act, still less by carping with academic critiques from safe sidelines. So, these questions are not to inhibit. They are simply one person's checklist for reflection on the run. (Throughout 'I' can also be 'we'.)

1 Should you draw up your own questions?

Yes, yes, yes ... yours should serve you better ... maybe when you have listed them you can encourage others to draw up and share theirs too ... still, here are some of mine.

2 What is in this for me?

What am I hoping to gain from this? What are my expectations? Am I putting my interests above those of participants?

3 What am I doing here?

QUESTIONS

Why here and not somewhere else? Why this community, workshop, course, class or group and not another? Why these people and not others?

4 Why do they think I am here?

Have I explained to them? Adequately?

5 What are their expectations?

What do they feel is in it for them? What fit or misfit is there between what I think they can expect and what they do expect? How can I help them to be realistic?

6 Who is participating in whose programme, project, workshop, course, class or group?

Who feels it is theirs? Are 'they' participating in mine or ours? Or am I, or are we, participating in theirs?

7 What are the significant 'axes of difference' in the community, workshop, course, class or group?

Gender? Age? Wealth? Social, ethnic or religious group? Education? Language or fluency? Technical ability? Or what? How do these combine?

8 Who are the lowers?

Who are marginalized or excluded? Those less fluent in the language? People who lack confidence? Females? Those of lower social, ethnic or religious status? Younger people and children? People with disabilities? The 'uneducated'? The very old? The poor...?

9 Who are the uppers?

Who are dominant? Those more fluent in the language? Those who are more confident? Males? Those of higher social, ethnic or religious status? Older people? The better educated? The relatively wealthy...?

10 Who are the stakeholders?

Who are the people affected or who might be affected by the process? Who are likely to gain? Who are likely to lose?

11 What is a good time and place for whom to meet?

When and where is convenient for them (especially lowers) to meet? Whose convenience takes precedence? Would it be better for them to meet on their own? Would they like me to go and come back later?

12 Who am I meeting and who am I not meeting?

Am I meeting uppers or lowers? Who is being left out? Who is not here? Why not? Where are they? What are they doing? Are they sick, weak, distant, busy working and earning, looking after others, socially excluded...? Would it be good to approach them and involve them? How?

13 What am I being told and shown, and what am I not being told and shown?

How does the person I am and how I am seen affect what people tell and show me? Do people think I could bring benefits or penalties? Are people being polite, prudent or deferential? Where am I going and not going? What am I being shown and not shown? What am I seeing and not seeing?

14 Is my behaviour empowering or disempowering?

What effects am I having on people, especially the lowers (those of lower status, weaker, less articulate...)? Will they be stronger, weaker and more or less able to stand up for themselves when I have finished?

15 How did I behave? (as a question to them)

And how should I behave? What should I do and not do?

16 What questions would 'they' (local people, participants, course, class or group members) like to ask me?

About myself? About my organization? About anything else?

17 What will happen after I leave?

What sort of process is likely to continue in the community, workshop, course, class or group? Who will follow up? Will anyone be penalized?

18 What have I left undone?

What did I miss, leave out? What remains to be done?

19 What am I now going to do?

What actions are needed? What are people now expecting? What commitments have I entered into? How can I fulfil these?

20 What lessons can I learn from this experience?

What would I do differently, knowing what I do now? What advice would I now give to others?

21 What other questions should be asked?

Part 2
Beginning, Middle and End

21 Ideas for Getting Started

[See also the 21s in **2** and **13**]

These are tips about the early stages of a participatory workshop, training or course. Bad starts can usually be overcome, but a good start helps a lot. Ideally, all have wanted to come, have prepared in advance, have arrived in good time, and are present at the start, satisfied with the logistical and financial arrangements, free from worries, and well rested, fit, friendly, open and enthusiastic.

Rarely indeed are all these conditions met for participants. In dealing with their absence in others it helps hugely if these conditions are met in you.

Contents

First things

1   Welcome and warm up
2   Checklist for starting
3   Expectations, hopes and fears
4   Hopes to learn and contribute
5   Objectives

Meeting, mixing and learning who we are

6   Meet and greet
7   Seed mixer
8   Bicycle chain
9   Mapping
10 Buses
11 Who are we? Raising hands or standing up
12 Short self-introductions
13 Mutual introductions
14 Time lines and rivers
15 Telling our stories
16 Name and throw
17 Remembering names

Preparing for the process

18 Making contracts
19 Teams for tasks
20 Agenda setting

Invent your own

21 Invent and share

FIRST THINGS

1 Welcome and warm up

Some ideas and tips:

- Think through what it must be like to be someone coming to the workshop, training or course. What problems or worries are they likely to have? Are there some who will have special problems? What can you do to help them? What can you ask others to do to help?

PARTICIPATORY FROM THE START

- Put up welcome notices.
- Be participatory from the start. Ask early comers to help. There are often things to do – moving chairs and tables, tearing up paper, finding someone who can make equipment work...
- If there are more than, say, ten people taking part, organize early comers to welcome others and ask them to give themselves name tags.
- Go for a relaxed and friendly start. Try to be free and relaxed yourself. What happens in the welcome and start can set the tone for the rest of the time.
- Make late arrivals welcome. Ask others to brief them on what has happened so far and to help them in other ways.

2 Checklist for starting

This is a checklist, not a sequence. Do things your own way, in whatever order makes sense to you.

- welcome
- administration and logistics
- expectations, hopes and fears (see 3 and 4 below)
- background and purpose (see 5 below)
- outline of the programme and/or process
- information – on documents, sources, videos, etc
- introductions (meeting, greeting, mapping, buses, etc) (see 6–17 below)
- contracts for behaviour (see 18 below)

5 : 1–2   21 IDEAS FOR GETTING STARTED

3 Expectations, hopes and fears

To encourage participants to think about what they expect, and to inform you, ask them what their expectations, hopes and fears are.

Options include

- As they arrive, ask them to take Post-its or cards, write down their expectations, and stick them up on a wall or board.
- Have separate Post-its or cards for hopes and for fears.
- Ask pairs or small groups to write expectations, or hopes and fears, on cards, one item to one card, which are then sorted on the ground, stuck up and displayed.
- Stick a large long sheet on a wall, with headings, columns and lines, for each person to fill in. The headings can be, for example, name, address and contact, and then any variety of details of expectations, hobbies, even personal symbol.

The expectations, hopes and fears can be addressed and commented on before starting. There are usually some humorous fears.

4 Hopes to learn and contribute

Invite participants to write on cards what they hope to learn and what they have to contribute. Take serious note of what they hope to learn.

Tips

- Ask for names to be written on all the cards. This enables you to try to meet individual needs, and to know who can be called on for what.
- Contributions can be great. They can also be too many, or embarrassingly inappropriate. Be cautious.

Some ways of handling them:

- Warn that there may not be enough time.
- Provide an open time when contributors can set up their stalls, or can hold discussions with whoever is interested.
- Run contributions as necessary in parallel.
- Make evening time available.
- Allow the group to set priorities for topics, presentations and discussions.

5 Objectives

It often helps to present or discuss objectives. Sometimes these have been outlined beforehand, in a notice or by letter. Sometimes objectives are best determined by the group.
Objectives preset. Judge whether to write them up and display them. In a good process objectives can change. Displaying preset objectives helps to maintain focus but makes change harder.

Objectives not preset. For a participatory process options include the following:

- Start with expectations. If these are on cards or Post-its, let them be grouped and summarized.
- Straight plenary discussion.
- Small groups discuss and report.
- Individual reflection and writing, followed by sharing in small groups, leading to plenary reports.
- Prioritize and select which objectives to address and which to postpone.

If you can summarize a consensus, well and good. If not, options include:

- leave differences unresolved;
- list the different objectives and let them coexist;
- plan part of the programme to have parallel sessions and topics to accommodate the differences;
- let a small group form to discuss further and make recommendations.

Take comfort in the thought that recognizing differences early on can pre-empt and prevent crises later.

MEETING, MIXING AND LEARNING WHO WE ARE

I do not recommend the exercise where you sit in a circle and go round, each naming all those who have gone before, so that the last person has to name everyone. This terrifies and humiliates those (like me) whose short-term memory is less than brilliant. Start instead with non-threatening activities like the following.

In all cases start with participants using big pens to write on sticky labels in bold capitals the name they want to be called. These are more personal, friendly and legible than the carefully typed names supplied by professional conference and workshop organizers.

6 Meet and greet

The simplest quick mixer. Sets a participatory tone of friendly edge-of-chaos right from the start. All walk around, greet (often shaking hands), and introduce themselves to everyone else.

Tips and options

- Start with everyone standing in an open space. Otherwise some may be left out or not take part.
- Indicate roughly how long each greeting and introduction should take.
- Remember that in some cultures women and men do not shake hands.
- If anyone is left out or not taking part go and greet them.

- If appropriate, suggest what information (eg name, organization) should be shared. Or each person states their favourite hobby and/or drink, film star, football club, etc (source: Kamal Kar).
- Give a time warning shortly before concluding.

Variant

Only greet those not already known. Simple, very effective and fun, spurning those already known. Excellent if a workshop involves people from different communities, organizations or courses some of whom already know one another.

Tip

Ask all to look around, see how many they already know, and raise hands to indicate the rough number. This makes them aware of who is present, and gives you an idea of how much new greeting there will be.

7 Seed mixer

A good way of starting a workshop, immediately establishing friendly relationships. Best for 10–30 participants but has been used for 40. At the end, everyone knows they have met and greeted everyone else.

Have ready:

- several piles of different sorts of seeds, beans, raisins, or similar counters, enough for each participant to have as many of them as there are participants (eg if there are 25 people, each will need 25 counters);
- plastic cups or glasses (two each) for those without pockets.

Allow 10–30 minutes, depending on numbers and how long greetings take.

1 Ask three or more people to count the participants and facilitators present. If they count different numbers (quite common) triangulate – cross-check to get closer to the right number.
2 Each person empties two pockets or picks up two containers.
3 Each counts out beans or whatever, all of the same sort, one for each person taking part (eg 18 people = 18 beans) and puts them in an empty pocket or container.
4 Indicate roughly how long each greeting and introduction should take.
5 Each then greets and says something to each other participant, exchanging a bean and placing the one received in the empty pocket or container

At the end, everyone should have one bean left. Who is that? And the other beans are a mixture of sizes and colours, symbolizing the mixing that has taken place

Tips and options

- Do not use if touching between women and men is a taboo for anyone.
- With two groups (say two university courses) coming together, each counts out only for the other group, not their own, and then exchanges only with those in the other group.
- Observe those who are being most talkative and invite them to speed up a bit.
- About two-thirds of the way through, warn how much time is left.
- If the counters are to be used again, and not made into a mixed bean stew, ask all to sort them at the end. Though therapeutic, it is time-consuming to do this oneself later.

Variant

In Sri Lanka, edible beans have been placed in the mouth (Mallika Samaranayake, personal communication).

8 Bicycle chain

Enables any number of participants to meet all the others quickly and informally. Excellent for large numbers (eg used with over 100 people in both Hyderabad and Bangalore).

Form two facing lines. Pair off. Each pair greets, says or asks whatever they wish. They then move off in opposite directions, like a bicycle chain, and greet whoever is next, continuing round at the ends. Keep going until all have met. This is when the chain has gone half way round.

Tips

- Find enough space for the chain to be roughly straight. This may be out of doors. With many people in a hot climate a shady road without traffic serves well.
- Indicate roughly how long each encounter should take. For large numbers (eg 100 people) you may need to keep it down to 10–20 seconds or the process may go on too long.
- Recommend saying the name of the other person (this helps memory).
- Brief participants to keep moving, and warn them to avoid a queue waiting on the other side to greet them. In India at least, congestion is common when one sequence of women meets another.
- With a large number, say over 60, appoint one non-participant to stand on each side with the task of (politely) easing traffic jams.

9 Mapping

A splendid ice-breaker, acceptable to even the stiffest group of senior bureaucrats. Draw and label, or imagine, a large map on the ground. Participants stand where they were born, and then move progressively to where they had (as applicable) primary, secondary and tertiary education, and then where their careers have taken them, ending where they are now.

What is shown is usually striking, even startling, and of interest to all.

Tips and options

- Can be indoors or outdoors.
- If no map has been drawn, give North and South and the position of one or two big places. Tell people to adjust to those near them. This works perfectly well.
- If a map is drawn, use chalk on cement, white powder on grass, tape on a road or on rocks, or simply labels, stones or symbols for places. It is not necessary to make the map geographically exact. It is more important to allow enough space where people are most likely to cluster.
- There may be scope for reflection on what is shown; for example, few participants from poor or isolated areas, or many from central cities.

Source: Thelma Trench

10 Buses

(The title comes from the way we get into different buses at a bus stand. Also known as *matatu* in Kenya, *dalla-dalla* in Tanzania, and quite likely *Tempo* in India and *Jeepney* in the Philippines.) An excellent active starter, easy to do, showing the composition of the group, and meeting and mixing with others with things in common.

Find space for free movement. Out of doors is good. If indoors, clear a space. Allow 10–30 minutes, depending on the number of categories and amount of discussion. People stand and cluster by category. Stress the need to shout out, seek others and move quickly.

Options for clusters include:

- *Mother tongue* (the language you grew up using). This can generate a pleasing diversity. The current known record is 36 mother tongues among 70 people, at Reading University in the UK. Further clustering can be those for whom the language of the workshop is their second or third or more language. This heightens awareness of the language advantages and disadvantages of participants, and the need for mutual consideration, clear and slow speech in the dominant language, and space and translations for those who wish to speak or listen in other languages.
- *Female/male.* If women or men are a marked minority, this can be noted and discussed. Note if women stand in a round bunch and men stand in a line more spaced out, as sometimes happens.
- *Discipline or profession.*
- *Type of organization.*
- *Special experience* (eg related to the topic of the workshop, training or course).
- *Travel time to reach the venue.* A circle is good with longest and shortest times next to one another.

- *Sign of the zodiac.* Name them (Aries, Taurus, Gemini, Cancer, Leo, Virgo, Libra, Scorpio, Sagittarius, Capricorn, Aquarius, Pisces) and point to a place for each. Each cluster can agree and shout out one of its characteristics. Fun.
- *Hobby or enthusiasm.* Good for meeting others with common interests.
- *Reason for coming to the workshop or course.* This can be both revealing and therapeutic.
- *Important issues.* What are the most important issues to be covered?

Tips and options

- Ask each group to shout out who they are.
- Invite observations on the groups, their size, what sorts are missing, etc, leading into reflective discussion. The balance between the sexes is often noteworthy.
- Have fun categories like the hour when you got up this morning.
- Ask participants to suggest categories (participatory but slightly risky!), and invent your own.
- End with a clustering which leads into the next activity.
- For some characteristics stand in a line between most and least (eg most and least experience or knowledge of a subject. This identifies those who need to learn and those who can help them to learn).
- Other diversities are *religion, race, ethnic group, class, caste, grade in an organization, salary* and *income.* If these are considered too sensitive, embarrassing or divisive, or inappropriate at the start, it is worth reflecting on why, and what could or should be done about it.

Source: Barbara Kaim, 1997

11 Who are we? Raising hands or standing up

Quicker but less interactive than buses. Can be used with any number including a big crowd in a hall. Good for getting a rough idea of who is present.

Ask for hands to be raised or for people to stand up, by groups, as for buses.

Tips and options

- Ask who you have missed.
- Point out how the group is composed so that all are aware. Identify significant sorts of people, organizations, professions etc that are under-represented or not present at all.
- Joke by asking, for example, for very unusual professions unlikely to be present, or by noting how some groups are sitting together, or in front, or on the fringes (which can be significant when women are a small minority).

12 Short self-introductions

For time-limited self-introductions. Going round the room with untimed self-introductions invites disaster. Following the law of expanding egos, and saying more when you have had more time to think about it, the first person soon after breakfast takes 20 seconds, but the last (it is now near lunchtime) 20 minutes. Here are three self-regulating ways to keep self-introductions short, so that you can relax without having to police the process.

Clap the long-winded

Anyone speaking longer than an agreed limit is applauded. Practise clapping. Introduce yourself at length (until there is clapping) to confirm. Then go round the room. (This can, however, lead to excessively short introductions.)

Time the next one

Agree a maximum time (anything from say one to five minutes). Write cards eg *1 minute left, 20 seconds left,* and *stop!* After introducing themselves, each person times the next person, and shows the cards as the time is up. (This is much to be recommended, including occasions when quite long self-introductions make sense. It regulates itself well.)

Strike a match

A box of matches is passed round. Each strikes one and can speak until it goes out. (Fun but wastes time if the matches are damp or a wind blows them out as in an open classroom in Tanzania.)

Tips and options

- Some people mumble. Do an inaudible self-introduction yourself. Suggest clapping, handraising or some other sign to be used by anyone who cannot hear.
- Ask each person to write their name on a large piece of paper and hold it up for all to see when introducing themselves.
- For *strike a match* get big matches if you want the introductions to be more than about 20 seconds.

13 Mutual introductions

Participants pair off, introduce themselves to each other, and then each introduces the other to the whole group. The pairs can be formed in different ways:

- random or self-selected;
- preset by the facilitator (two cards for each pair, one name on either side, can be picked up, and pairs find one another);
- deliberate diversity mix: eg one person who has been at an earlier workshop, and one who has not, or one woman and one man, one old and one young, one from the field and one from headquarters;
- hat selection: each person writes personal details (eg date of birth, height, favourite colour, favourite drink, hobby and favourite film star) on a piece of paper, the pieces of paper are folded and mixed in a hat, each person draws one and searches for the originator. Fun (*Source:* Kamal Kar).

Variant

This can be done with threes instead of pairs – A introduces B, B introduces C and C introduces A.

Warnings

With a large group this can take a long time and become tedious. There is also a danger of trying so hard to think and remember what one is going to say that others' introductions are not listened to.

14 Time lines and rivers

Good for reflection on events leading up to a workshop. You need flip charts and pens.

Personal time line

Invite each participant to prepare a personal time line, listing in sequence the events that led to their coming to the workshop, draw this on a flipchart, and then share it with others. A self-portrait or other personal information are other options on the flip chart.

Group time lines

One or more groups construct time lines (or 'rivers') on the ground representing the evolution of the subject of the workshop, training or course. (At the First Global REFLECT Conference at Puri in Orissa, India, in November 1998 groups by continent made 'rivers' on the sand of the sea shore to represent their history of participation, and then presented these to each other.)

River of life

Ask each to draw a river of their life on a flip chart, showing big things that mattered and changed direction, or whatever else they wish. The rivers are then displayed and/or presented in small groups. This can be a powerful personal learning about oneself as well as about others. Allow enough time – usually at least 20 minutes for the drawing.

15 Telling our stories

For self-introductions to small groups. Each participant in the group has a sheet with questions on which to make notes. The sheet may say, for example:

'Take two minutes to prepare to introduce yourself to the rest of your table group by answering the following questions:

1   Who am I, what is my job right now, how long have I worked in the organization, and what other jobs have I had?
2   Why am I interested in the topic of the workshop, training or course?

3   What do I see as the most important issues to be covered?'

Each makes notes on the sheet, and then has a time limit for self-introduction to the group.

Tip

Each group should appoint a timekeeper.

Source: Matthias zur Bonsen

16 Name and throw

To help learn one another's names in an enjoyable and non-threatening manner. Suitable for groups of up to about 20 or 25.

   You need: big, legible name labels, a rubber ball (or ball of string for the variant). Ensure everyone's name tags are visible from a distance. Stand in a circle. Whoever holds the ball calls out the name of another and throws the ball to her or him. She or he then does the same for someone who has not yet had the ball. Continue until everyone has taken part.

Variant

Use a ball of string, holding the string. At the end there will be a web connecting everyone.

17 Remembering names

Ways of helping to remember each other's names.

   Each has a large name sticker. Ask each person to think how others can remember their name and something about themselves.

Ideas

* the origin and meaning of the name;
* something about how it is used or has been used;
* a personal distinguishing feature;
* a passion, enthusiasm or hobby.

This can be done standing in a circle and taking turns.

Tips and options

* Each steps forward and acts their passion, enthusiasm or hobby.
* Use the bicycle chain (see 8 above) for all to discuss, one by one in pairs, how they can remember each other's names:
    'xxxxx, I am going to remember you are XXXXX because/by your... '.
    'You can remember my name is YYYYY because/by my...'
(Many variations are possible – invent and share your own.)

Sources: Andrea Cornwall and others

PREPARING FOR THE PROCESS

18 Making contracts

Four sorts of contracts can be negotiated for establishing norms of behaviour and conduct. They involve participants, which includes workshop *participants*, course members and students, and *facilitators*, which includes workshop facilitators, trainers, faculty, lecturers and teachers.

Between participants

Topics can include mutual help, restraining big talkers and helping the silent speak [see **19**]. Team contracts are good for fieldwork. Teams discuss and list their code of behaviour.

Tips

- Codes are written up and displayed.
- Codes include how to deal with deviant behaviour.

Between all – participants and facilitators

Each group can draw up norms and behaviours for the other, and then discuss and negotiate. Or they can alternate in proposing single points.

Tips

- Timing is a common issue. Some prefer to leave timing open-ended, especially in a workshop where sessions may go on well into the night. Others prefer stricter timing. Get a sense of how much flexibility is acceptable. A good participatory workshop or training often works best if it can go on 'over time'. But this cannot happen when there are other timebound commitments (children to fetch from nursery, other meetings or classes, public transport schedules, another group coming to use the room!).
- If, like me, you are bad at keeping to time, a public commitment to finish at a certain hour helps as a discipline.

Participants' code for facilitators

Participants draw up a code for how they would like facilitators to behave. A neat reversal of power which sets a good precedent for participation.

Facilitators' own contract

A facilitators' team can have its own contract. An example drawn up by a team of four was:

- be direct but nice;
- meet each day at 8.30pm;

- give honest and constructive feedback;
- be open to constructive criticism;
- if two facilitators agree that something is not going well, they should show a time-out sign to the active facilitator who should consult them when appropriate;
- add-ons to explanations given by the active facilitator are acceptable;
- punctuality;
- make use of different team strengths but also help others to learn your strengths.

Source: John Gaventa and Heidi Attwood, 1998

19 Teams for tasks

Ask volunteers to sign up for tasks and responsibilities for the workshop, training or course. In a workshop these can include:

- entertainment;
- food;
- evaluation (can be daily, to start each new day);
- energizers;
- feedback to facilitators.

The teams then determine much of what happens and how, and deal with problems themselves. This takes a load off you. It also gives you swift feedback when problems are arising.

20 Agenda setting

A workshop, training or course can be anything from fully planned to fully open. Participatory planning and flexibility usually pay off. Here are two examples. *Blank sheet* can take quite some time. *Group listing* (and scoring) can be remarkably quick.

Blank sheet

The Asian Health Institute in Japan starts a five-week course by giving participants a blank sheet. The programme is then built up from what they want and what the faculty have to offer.

Group listing

In a workshop, all write on cards, one item to one card, topics they hope will be addressed. All take part in sorting the cards into categories. These are then displayed and discussed. Arrange the programme to cover the items.

Options and tips

- Cards are scored for priority. Each participant has a ration of small stickers, or marks to be made with a pen. Scoring systems vary: I favour a fixed number per person (say seven) which they can allocate however they like (eg one on each of seven cards, or four on one, two on another and one on a third). Spread the cards to make space for several people to score at the same time.
- If there are to be parallel discussion groups, categories with roughly equal scores will usually attract roughly equal numbers of participants.
- If there are too many groupings, see if some apply across others. Make a matrix with topics on one axis, and crosscutting themes on the other.

Examples

- At Thakani, Nepal, it only took half an hour for 25 people to identify and agree the agenda for a four-day PRA retreat. All wrote on cards and then sorted them on the ground.
- At Tarangire in Tanzania, permanent secretaries wrote on cards to set the discussion agenda for a two-day retreat. The cards were then sorted by the facilitators during a break.
- In a PRA network meeting in Pakistan, seven topics emerged from a ground sort of cards. Three of these were seen to be themes (eg networking) which applied across the other four. We ended up with four topic groups, each of which considered how the three themes applied to their topic.

INVENT YOUR OWN

21 Invent and share

Innovate, develop your own ways of getting started and share what you do with others.

21 Energizers

There are times when energy levels fall and attention flags. Towards the end of a morning is one bad time. The early afternoon after lunch is worse: the 'graveyard session'. Other difficult times come with heavy presentations, dull topics, excessive heat and terminal saturation. Try to avoid these.

Bad times can be moderated with activities and energizers.

Activities are part of the process and rhythm of a workshop, training or course. Put the harder, less active things at the better times, and easier and more active ones at the worse times. Intersperse activities like 1 to 4 below: they are as obvious as they are underused. They energize without being called energizers. [See **5**; **11**; **15**; and **18**].

HOUR AFTER LUNCH

Energizers themselves (5 to 21 below) do more than wake up. They are fun in their own right, and break ice and melt it. They can become part of the participatory culture of a workshop, training or course. In an extended training in Tanzania for a mix of academics, consultants, government staff and students of several nationalities the energizer games were later seen as a key factor in breaking down barriers and bringing the very different sorts of people together.

There are many, many energizers. Their global epicentre is the Philippines: the Filipino proliferation could fill a book. They can be improvised. You can ask participants to provide some. Beware, though, of long ones with little activity.

Tips

- Respect those who do not want to take part.
- With any group that is stiff at first, start gently and gradually work up.
- Take part and set an example yourself.
- Be sensitive to culture, gender and disability. For cultures or contexts where physical contact between women and men is not acceptable there are plenty

of energizers which do not involve touching. Some energizers marginalize those with disabilities: consult them beforehand and, where you can, give them roles as observers, judges or umpires.

- If people are tired you may ask 'do we need an energizer?' and be greeted by 'NO!!!'. Don't be dismayed. Saying 'NO!!!' itself wakes up. Shouted louder and louder it gets more and more air into the lungs. And to justify denying the need some may struggle more to stay alert.

Contents

A PART OF PROCESS

1 Buzz

So easy. So underused. Invite participants to buzz with others next to them – about what has just been covered or done, an issue that has arisen, the agenda... The immediate wake-up often includes learning by talking.

2 You move, all move

Simple and natural. Change your position. If you are talking, go to another part of the room and talk from there. Most of those not already asleep will shift in their seats, or bend their necks.

Put up posters round the room, and invite all to get up, walk over and stand while you show and talk about them. The movement gets the circulation going.

Folklore has it that only horses can sleep while standing up. Though Japanese commuters appear to have developed this skill, I have never observed it in a workshop situation.

YOU MOVE, ALL MOVE

3 Form groups

Simple, quick and functional. Form groups to discuss a topic or for an activity. To mix and move for buzzes ask for pairs or threes; for example with people:

- not known to one another;
- from other parts of the room;
- from other sorts of organization (or the same sort);
- from other disciplines (or the same one).

For other ways to form groups see **11**:4, Jungle, which is a brilliant way to energize and form random groups, capable of retrieving even the most torpid afternoon, for a time at least.

4 Games and role plays

Wonderful scope for active engagement and creativity. Games and role plays are best when they fit the theme and foster the learning of the workshop. [See **14**; **18**; and **19** – see also **15**:10].

Tip

If you are timid, as I am, about risking a role play, and dithering whether to dare, be a devil and give it a go. Role plays by participants usually go better, sometimes brilliantly better, than you expect.

GENTLER

5 Gentle rain

Peaceful. Good with a large group. Ask everyone to follow you in tapping the palm of one hand with one finger of the other hand; then two fingers; then three; then four; then the whole hand; and then back again down to one. People end up smiling.

6 Numbers

Gentle fun. Stand in a circle. Count in turn round the circle. Anyone with a multiple of five claps hands instead of saying the number. Anyone with a multiple of seven or a number with a seven in it, turns around once instead of saying the number. Those who make mistakes drop out.

NUMBERS

The numbers and the actions can be varied in many ways; for example, less actively by saying a word instead of the number, or more actively by sitting on the ground.

7 Swatting mozzies

Easy, quick. The room is full of mosquitoes. They are all around us and landing and biting. Swat them with your hands – in front, down by your ankles, behind your head, on your face, to the left, to the right...by your neighbour... (*on* your neighbour...?)

Option

At the same time make mozzie noises, and shout 'got it' (in various languages).

8 Body writing

A good progressive loosener. Write your name with parts of the body. Make up your own sequence. Options include:

* right finger;
* left finger;
* right elbow;
* left elbow;
* and so on through big toes, knees, shoulders, nose and finally belly button.

This involves a surprising amount of exercise, especially the belly button which is good to end on. Ears, Adam's apples and other socially acceptable bits of the anatomy are other options.

Tip

Do them all yourself, especially the belly button at which stage for some participants laughter may substitute for action.

9 Get up and do something

Simple and effective. From gentle to energetic some of the endless options are:

- what in North America is called a comfort break (more direct expressions available in other languages);
- stand up and stretch;
- wiggle or rotate toes, heel, knees, elbows ...
- put hands behind backs and bend further and further forward;
- change seats, maybe with someone at the other end of the room;
- jump up and down, do exercises;
- go outside, fetch something ...
- walk round the building (make it a race?);
- throw snowballs, weather permitting;
- a Cossack dance;
- stand on your head;
- and so on.

MORE ENERGETIC

10 Mirrors

Fun. Pair off. One person is the actor, the other the mirror. The mirror does whatever the actor does, mirroring the actions. Continue for a couple of minutes and then reverse roles. Demonstrate with a partner to set an example with appropriate vigour.

MIRRORS

11 Elephant, giraffe, toaster

Fun and likely to make everyone laugh. Stand in a circle. Demonstrate the different positions for three people. For elephant, the middle person uses an arm for the trunk (a nice option is to cross arms and hold the nose with the non-trunk arm) and those on either side raise their elbows for ears. For giraffe, the middle person puts an arm up in the air and those on either side put one leg forward. For toaster, those on either side join hands and the middle person jumps up and down like toast.

Stand in the middle of the circle. Turn around, point to someone and say either elephant, giraffe or toaster. The person pointed to is the middle person. The three immediately act the word. Any one of the three who hesitates or gets it wrong takes your place in the centre and repeats.

Tip

Invent your own variations to fit conditions and cultures.

12 Picking fruit

Non-violent, using lots of different muscles.

'We are going to pick fruit (oranges, apples, *jamun*... whatever) from a tree. Together with me, lift up a ladder and put it on your shoulder. Pick up a basket. Walk over to the tree. Put the ladder against the tree. Climb the ladder. Careful. Hang the basket on a small branch. Start picking. Reach far to the right. Then far to the left. The basket is filling up. It is getting heavy. OH NO! THE BRANCH HAS BROKEN AND THE BASKET HAS FALLEN. THE FRUIT IS ALL OVER THE GROUND. Climb down the ladder. Get down on the ground and pick up the fruit and put it back in the basket. Some have rolled far away. Get them all. There are more over there. Now you have them all. Put the ladder on your shoulder. Pick up the basket – it's heavy. Carry them home and put them away.'

13 Anilbhai (or anyone else) says...

An old favourite. Stand in a circle. Give instructions – to jump up and down, to touch toes, to kneel down, to turn around, to stop, etc. Participants only follow the instructions when you say 'Anilbhai says...', but not when you simply command. Do several 'Anilbhai says...' and then one without. Those who make mistakes drop out.

14 Song and dance

Fine when the context is right. Singing can be good: it gets air into the lungs and gives a good feeling all round. Songs that everyone knows, and with a good refrain, are best. Beware of extended virtuoso solos. To energize well, all need to sing.

   Dance invigorates and breaks barriers of behaviour. Dance can be to clapping, singing or improvised drumming. All can dance or can stand in a circle taking turns in the centre. Some can involve others in dances from different traditions and cultures.

15 All move who...

Another easy old favourite. Stand, or sit on chairs, in a circle, with one person (yourself first) in the middle. Say 'All move who...' and then add, for example:

- are wearing something blue;
- travelled more than a day to get here;
- can speak two or more languages;
- got up this morning before 6.00am;
- had xxxxx for breakfast;
- and so on.

ALL MOVE WHO...

Those concerned move to a space left by someone else. The person left in the middle gives another 'All move who ...'

Tip

If all the choices are to do with clothing (quite common), be slow when you have to move so that you are left in the middle yourself, and then say something quite different.

16 Progressive greeting (ending back to back)

Clear a space. All stand with hands behind backs, looking at the ground. Walk around, weaving in and out, but not meeting others' eyes. Now allow your arms to swing. Now greet only with your eyes as you pass...and so on through smiling, slapping hands, shaking hands, bumping elbows, feet, knees and finally (depending on the group) hip to hip, nose to nose, and back to back or bottom to bottom.

Tip and option

- Be gender and culturally sensitive in how far you go.
- Speed up with jogging.

Source: Kate Norrish and Rachel Searle-Mbullu

17 Racing round

Good quick fun when seated in a circle, hollow square or U. All stand up and are given numbers. Odd numbers are to move clockwise and even numbers anticlockwise (or vice versa). Odd numbers raise hands, and then even numbers raise hands, to ensure they know which direction to go in. When you say 'go' all run round racing to be the first back.

Variants

Weaving. All weave in and out as they go round. Tell everyone to start by going to the left of the first person they pass, then to the right of the second, and so on. A fair degree of amiable chaos can be anticipated.

The Atebelle Walk. An advanced energizer, not for beginners. I know I should not include it but the temptation is too strong. It was invented in desperation at The Art of Facilitation Workshop held at Atebelle near Bangalore in 1996, at eight in the evening. All were exhausted and thirsty. The session was to continue for 20 more minutes. The bar was open but not yet patronized. Only an extreme remedy could meet the need of the hour.

Place chairs in a circle. Remove shoes. Climb up on the chairs, number and proceed as above, walking round on the chairs. A good deal of physical contact is involved. Gender and cultural sensitivity are in order. Men and women could have separate circles. A tame version would be for all to move in the same direction.

Tip

Warn that this is at the participants' own risk.

18 As and Bs

A really good one. Stand in a circle. Ask everyone to look around and pick another person, and to raise a hand when they have done that. That other person is their A. Then ask everyone to pick a second person and raise a hand. That second person is their B.

When you say 'go', each gets as close as they can to their A and as far away as they can from their B. Then reverse it – close to B and far from A.

Tips

- Stress the need for speed.
- Stress keeping far away from B as well as close to A.

19 Rat (or mouse), snake, lion

Remove shoes.

'We are going to go for a walk in the forest. Whenever I say rat, jump up on a chair and scream (all practise). Whenever I say snake, throw back your arms, draw in your breath in horror (all practise). Whenever I say lion, crouch down, cover your head and groan (all practise).'

Make up a story. Here is an example:

'One day I was walking through the beautiful forest. The birds were singing. The wind was rustling in the leaves. Nature was peaceful and friendly. Then on the path in front I saw, suddenly – a *snake*. It was gliding along stealthily. I wondered where it was going. Then I saw it was stalking a *rat*. The *snake* was getting closer and closer, and I thought it would catch its prey, when there was another noise. And there, coming through the bushes, was a *lion*. The *rat* heard the *lion* and ran away. The disappointed *snake* gave up and wriggled away. The *lion* saw the *snake* and made off back into the trees. And so the forest was peaceful again and I continued my walk.'

Tips

Judge the capacity of the group. Some may not find it easy to jump on a chair. Do not mention the animals too many times or participants will collapse exhausted.

Source: Ernesto Cloma

20 Cats and dogs

Third degree. Possibly the most energizing energizer of all. This requires a clean open space. When chairs are in a circle, the space enclosed may be adequate, but more space does no harm. Only attempt with willing parties of reasonably mobile physique and playful disposition. Any who opt out can be asked to observe and see fair play.

Participants are divided into a minority of dogs (one–three is enough) with the rest as cats. All get down on all fours. Dogs practise barking and cats miaowing. Then barking dogs chase miaowing cats trying to touch their feet (or another agreed part of the body). Cats touched by dogs stop miaowing, become dogs, start barking and chase the remaining cats. Continue until no cats remain.

Tip

If the workshop is being videoed, video this.

21 Collect, invent and improvise your own

Make your own collection. Invent. Make up a story with actions that go with it. Set up a race or competition. Improvise. Be yourself. Choose energizers that suit your style.

21 Ideas for Evaluation and Ending

Terminal trauma

Why is it so easy to write about this?

'What are we going to do about evaluation?' 'Which of us can do it?' On the last day, or in the last hour. We have not thought it out. And then it is rushed, or not done at all.

What happens? Everyone is tired. It is late afternoon or early evening. If it is hot, it is very hot. If there are mosquitoes, it is their mealtime and many maraud. The participatory parts of the programme were so good – we could not have stopped them in their tracks. And there was no way we could have shut up 'Old Big Mouth', the recognized authority (recognized by Himself) once he had started. And that visiting professor who talked about active listening deep into the lunch hour. So we are late. What to do? The clock ticks. It is past the agreed time to end. One or two have already slipped out (to pick up children, to catch a bus, train or plane, to honour an appointment, or because they have had enough). Others fidget or furtively frown at their watches. Minds stray to home, family, in-tray, bar or bed. So, limit damage. Abandon reflection. Dispense with evaluation. Cut losses and conclude before anyone else leaves. Anyway, perhaps it's as well. The evaluations would have been bad when everyone was so exhausted and fed up. And then we might never have been asked again.

This happens. Well, it has happened to me. It is a shame. It misses chances to learn and improve; for participants through reflection, and for facilitators through feedback. So:

Tips

Write reflection and evaluation into the programme. Then it will be harder to forget them or leave them out. Consider emphasizing reflection [see **16**:19].

Allow enough time. Evaluation is usually squeezed. Discuss how long you think you need, and then double it.

Plan the ending sequence backwards. Plan time use from the finishing time backwards to a flexible point in the programme. Then make sure you go into the final routine on time.

Energize and relax. Try to help everyone feel alert and at ease. A short fun energizer often makes sense.

Choices. Reflection can precede evaluation.

This can be:
- individual or group
- personal or shared
- written or thought
- and/or combined in various sequences [**16**]

Evaluations can be:
- written or spoken
- public or private
- open-ended or closed
- group or individual
- authored or anonymous
- and/or combined in various sequences

PLAN BACKWARDS

Those that follow are some good and useful combinations. There are surely many more.

Contents

Evaluation

Ending

EVALUATION

Why evaluate?

The usual overt purposes are:

- for facilitators to learn;
- to help participants learn, and share and consolidate their learning.

An occasional covert purpose is:

- to gain testimonials for consultant facilitators' brochures.

(Some professionals 'faciPULate' their clients onto a high before the evaluation. Once as a client I had this done to me. I gave a rave assessment. Later I wanted to retract. But it was too late. And the facilitator lost while winning because he missed an opportunity to learn from what I might have said.)

General Tip

If a detailed evaluation by sessions is sought, precede it with a recap. A good way is to have outputs or a summary around the walls of the room, and walk round together and talk it through before doing the evaluation. Otherwise details from the earlier sessions are easily overlooked.

1 Daily monitoring and feedback

It is good practice to have daily monitoring and feedback. Some of the more common forms, which can be separate or combined, are:

- *Mood meter.* Post up a chart in a public place, perhaps near the door. Its columns are workshop days, and its lines either three or five indicating levels of morale or satisfaction. Each line can 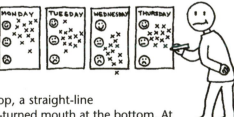 have a face – a big smile at the top, a straight-line mouth in the middle, and a down-turned mouth at the bottom. At the end of each day participants mark with pen or sticker to show how they feel (or it can be, for example, how much they learnt). This provides a quick check and feedback, and an early warning if things are not going well or some are dissatisfied.

MOOD METER

See also *VIPP: Visualisation in Participatory Programmes* (McKee et al, 1993, p129) [see **21**:14].

- *Evening feedback.* A few participants can be chosen or volunteer to solicit feedback and suggestions and pass these to the facilitators at their evening meeting. Problems can then usually be known and handled quickly. One option is for feedback team members to wear badges during the day on which they will be reporting.
- *Next day feedback.* Reflection on highlights of the day before and what was learnt can be a good start for a new day. One, two or three participants start each day with a review of the day before. Each day can have a different team, and each can choose its own form of feedback. Set a time limit, and discourage a blow-by-blow recapitulation.

2 Verbal

Ask for verbal comments. Remember that the purpose is learning, by yourselves and by participants.

Strengths

- requires little or no preparation;
- can be reflective and helpful, articulating and reinforcing what has been learnt.

Weaknesses

- can converge on an unbalanced collective trajectory which goes up or down, towards either ecstatic enthusiasm or morbid melancholy;
- facilitators may become defensive;
- usually only some people speak, often those with the strongest views;
- can run on and be difficult to finish.

Tips

- Set a time limit.
- Start with what *you*, as facilitator, have learnt. This can set the tone, with frank recognition of any major errors, expressing these in the positive form of lessons learnt, and perhaps asking advice for the future.
- Affirm criticism and show that you understand.
- Don't manipulate to get a favourable evaluation. You will learn less, and participants will be irritated. We remember and resent occasions when we have been manipulated.

Option

- Set a framework, for example, one negative comment, one positive and one learning, from each person (but this takes time). Take the negatives first, then the positives, then the learning.

3 Scribbled on the spot

Write up some basic questions on a flip chart and ask participants to write replies. This is quick and easy. The questions chosen depend on the purpose. If this is for you to learn, the following may serve:

- Were your expectations met?
- What did you find most useful?
- What did you find least useful?
- What did you learn? (or What did you get out of this workshop?)
- What if anything will you do in follow-up?
- How could a workshop like this be improved?

I used to ask the first three and the last. But the last three can be asked on their own: 'what did you learn?' reinforces learning through early recall, 'what will you do?' focuses on action, and 'how to improve?' makes criticism easy. Usually there are surprises and a lot to learn from the replies.

4 Questionnaire with scoring

Scoring each session or segment. One–five (five scores) or zero–five (six scores) are common and convenient. Other aspects like logistics, food and entertainment can be included. The criterion or criteria can vary. Options for evaluation of the content of a workshop can include one or more of:

- useful
- learning
- enjoyable

Leave a space for general comments.

5 Cards

Participants write their comments on cards, one comment per card. Big pens and capital letters keep it short and clear.

Tips and options

- With large numbers limit the cards per person or per group.
- With small numbers there is no need to limit the number of cards.
- Coloured cards can be used to differentiate points that are negative, those that are positive and learning.
- Work individually, in small groups or in pairs. Talking first in pairs followed by individual writing usually works well.
- Sort the cards on the ground/display on a wall.
- In summarizing, start with negative, then positive and finally learning.
- Discuss/ask about some cards.
- Invite participants to rank or score the cards (easiest with stickers or pens, and a fixed number of marks per person).

6 Evaluation wheel

Draw a large circle on a flip chart, or flip charts joined together. Mark in equal sized sectors with lines from centre to circumference, and label each sector for one aspect of evaluation (eg logistics, food, facilitation, fieldwork). Each participant does likewise on a piece of paper, and evaluates each sector by drawing a line from the centre. A long line to the circumference is excellent. No line at all is dismal beyond despair. When they have finished, participants in turn draw in their evaluations on the big chart. This ends up with many lines in each sector, giving a clear visual evaluation which also indicates the range of views for each aspect.

EVALUATION WHEEL AND
SPIDER DIAGRAMS

Tips and options

*   Brainstorm at the beginning to establish the categories for the sectors and how many they should be.
*   The facilitators can be absent, or the chart can be out of their sight, so that they do not see who draws what length of line.
*   It may be best used together with another method that elicits detail.
*   Criteria can be spokes of a wheel, leading to a spider diagram (see diagrams).

Source: Jennifer Rietbergen-McCracken in *Participatory Learning and Action: A Trainer's Guide* [see **21**:1, p213].

7 Stand to score

Quick, flexible, active and good when tired at the end of a day. Ask participants to stand between two poles to indicate their evaluation.

Tips and options

*   Ask why people have chosen their position.
*   Go through the programme, standing for each part.
*   Score by putting the numbers zero–ten on a wall or on the floor.
*   Ask participants what else they would like to score.

Positions and scores are likely to be influenced by others' movements, and by awareness of facilitators if they are watching. All the same, those at the low ends usually have good insights to share which provide valuable feedback.

Source: Patta Scott-Villiers

8 Visual scoring

Draw one or more charts, or invite participants to draw these, with aspects, sessions or topics to be evaluated. List these down the left-hand side, and put scores or ranks across the top. Decide or ask what aspect or question is to be evaluated. Examples are:

- How useful did you find ...?
- Was there too little or too much time for ...?'
- How much did you learn ....?

Then each person enters a score, with a dot or cross with pen or sticker, for each item.

How much did you learn... ? has the advantage of actually enhancing learning through reflection and recall as participants think through the sessions.

Tips and options

- If time is short place the chart by the exit and ask participants to complete it on leaving. Any who leave early can fill it in before going.
- Can be used to revisit hopes and fears.
- Can provide the basis for discussion. No one has to take responsibility for a high or low score. This makes criticism easy ('I suppose one reason why that got a low score was ...') without it being an individual judgement.
- Scores can be plus or minus, or zero–five, or on other scales.
- Each participant can draw a graph through the days and sessions on the x axis against a score (eg zero–ten) on the y axis (*Source:* Pike and Selby [see **21**:17] citing Coover et al, 1997)

For several variants see **21**:14, pp133–5.

9 Step forward or back

All stand in a line. As each activity, session, dimension or experience is named, they step forwards for positive or backwards for negative to show their assessment. Dimensions can include, for example, gender sensitivity, the language used, the teaching/learning techniques, the environment, incidents or the facilitation. The question against which the assessment is made needs to be specified, for example:

'Did you feel empowered, or disempowered, by ...?'
'How much did you learn from ...?'

Tips and options

- Recording needs to be very alert. One person can count those who step back, and another those who step forwards, and by how much, for each item.

- A less active variant is thumbs up, thumbs down, and wiggling thumbs for so-so (*Source:* Pike and Selby [see **21**:17] citing Coover et al, 1997).
- Ask participants what the criteria should be.

Source: Concept Group at the First Global REFLECT Conference, Puri, Orissa, India, November 1998

10 Free matrix scoring

Participants list what they wish to evaluate, list their criteria and matrix score. This can be done individually or in groups [see **15**:7]. An advantage is the diversity and range of aspects or events that are evaluated, and the diversity and range of criteria. Disadvantages are that what comes from different groups will not be comparable. Groups are also likely to take longer than with preset matrix scoring.

11 Preset matrix scoring

The matrix is made out in advance so that all participants have to do is score the boxes. This is quicker and more comparable, so that overall averages can be worked out. (Both forms of matrix scoring give participants something to put in their reports on a workshop, training or course.)

Tips

- The categories and criteria can be elicited from participants rather than determined by facilitators.
- For later averaging, ask all groups to score from the same number (usually five or ten).

(*Source:* District Sector Staff workshop, Shinyanga, Tanzania, November 1997.)

12 Facilitators' own evaluation and learning

The main purpose of evaluation is learning. It is easy to fail here. It is tempting to reject criticism without understanding it, and without seeing the lessons to be learnt. So as facilitators we do well to make time, among ourselves, to reflect and learn at the end so that we can do better next time.

Tips

- This can be systematic, going through participants' evaluations, collating, counting and assessing.
- Alternatively, it can be convivial, depending on culture, custom and consumption habits, over a beer, soda, coffee, cup of tea or, in Scotland, whisky or, in Kyrgyzstan, vodka. Enjoy.

ENDING

The certificate snare

There is often a demand for certificates after a workshop, training or course. With some training workshops organizers spring on you, near the end, a beautifully printed set of certificates, which includes your name and a place for you to sign. Oh dear. With PRA-related workshops I have decided I will not sign them.

Three main things can be wrong with signing certificates:

1   *The certificate culture* in which appearances are valued more than reality. People take part less to learn and change and more to get the piece of paper.
2   *Deception.* Some get the spirit of PRA and participation quickly and its behaviour and attitudes. Others think they have it, but have not. Others sense they have not got it and it is not for them. There is no way of separating out who is who. In any case, giving certificates to some and not others would be a horrendous way to end. But if all receive them, they are debased and some will give a false impression. Quite simply, certificates mislead.
3   *Abuse.* There is no control on how certificates are used. All are free to photocopy them, add them to their CVs, frame them on their office walls and use them in job applications.

CERTIFICATE SNARE

Opinions differ about solutions. A refuses to sign certificates at all. B will sign them only after feedback on follow-up. C will sign a 'certificate of attendance' which simply says that the person was there. But there are two neat solutions. Both need careful anticipation.

13 The pledge certificate

A South African innovation. The original certificate is self-explanatory. It read:

---

*Community Consultation and Facility Management Workshop,
Sebokeng,*

16–24 November 1999

This is to certify that

I,...

attended the above workshop. In so doing, I have pledged to:

....

....

....

SIGNED   [participant]

....

SIGNED   [Barbara Masakela, Deputy Chairperson
                      SA Sports Commission]

....

SIGNED   [Peter Bryant, Manager
                      UK/SA Sports Initiative]
                      Supported by: DfID, UK South Africa Sports Initiative, South
                      African Sports Congress

Source: Kamal Singh

---

14 Group photograph and farewell certificates

I like these.

Group photograph certificate. There is a group photograph for everyone. These are best mounted on paper with a margin for writing on. The photos are passed round. Everyone signs each photo. If there is time and space personal messages can be included.

Source: Regional Participation Workshop, Amman, October 1997.

Farewell certificate. A robust piece of paper is fixed to the back of each person. All move around and write messages of appreciation and farewell on the backs of others. This gives everyone a very personal memento and reminder to take home.

Source: James Mascarenhas

15 Final questions and issues

Questions and issues may have been collected as the workshop, course or session has gone on. These are best written on cards, in capitals, and stuck up where they can be seen (adhesive spray, or small rolls of masking tape, are good). Arrange these by subject. Write up the heading for each to stand out boldly in another colour or form.

It is often best to deal with these at intervals during a workshop rather than let them accumulate towards the end. Participants can be invited to pick issues that they will handle. Or groups can form, discuss and present back. Even so, there may be questions and issues left over where participants would like an input from the facilitator, trainer or teacher. The ideal may still be to deal with these in a participatory way. But time may be against you.

This is perilous. It puts you in the position of the person who is meant to know, while others do not. There are dangers of preaching and prattling on and on. The end of a participatory workshop is not a time to pontificate. It is a time to be focused, succinct and forward-looking [see 13:19]. If you simply have to talk and respond, here are some tips:

- Find a time-keeper to shut you up.
- Ask participants to mark (eg each person allocated five or seven or whatever number of marks) those cards that are most important. Deal only or mainly with those with higher marks.
- Write short sound-bite comments on some of the cards. This can sharply reduce presenting time.
- Ask participants to mark cards where they have a comment to make. Call on them as you get to the card.
- Refer to accessible written sources.
- When stumped, answer one question with 'use your own best judgement'.
- Refer to 21 ways to not answer a question. Whoever wishes can score you for answering and not answering.

Variant

Instead of having cards in advance, set aside time for a final discussion. Invite reflective comments. Write each topic on a card as it comes up. Stick up and order the cards as you go. When enough have come, give your own brief reactions. (This can work really well, especially if seating is muddled up with low eye contact so that people feel freer to talk and raise issues.)

16 The Margolis wheel

An intense and good experience to come near the end. This enables participants to share and receive advice on real problems and opportunities. It reinforces solidarity and mutual support. It can also surprise people with their own ability to counsel others.

You need four–six pairs of chairs, facing each other, arranged in a circle. As many circles of pairs of chairs as fit the number taking part [see **12**]. Allow ten minutes for briefing and reflection, plus:

4 pairs of chairs	25–30 minutes
5 pairs of chairs	30–35 minutes
6 pairs of chairs	35–40 minutes

1   Ask participants to reflect and choose a problem or opportunity they face or will face. This can be in their work and/or when they return to their institutions, or be any personal problem on which they would like advice. Stress that everything that passes is in confidence between friends.
2   Ask everyone to sit in a chair, any chair. Those on the inner ring are counsellors, and those on the outer ring their clients. There are three minutes only for each round of advice, roughly one minute for posing the problem, and two minutes for the advice
3   After two minutes warn that only one minute is left. After three minutes, all the outer ring move one seat in the same direction. The inner ring, of counsellors, stays put. Repeat the procedure.
4   When the outer ring has gone round, counsellors and clients swap seats. The process is repeated with the roles changed.

Tips and options

* Encourage note-taking, otherwise much will be forgotten. Notes can be taken on the run, or two minutes or so can be set aside at the end of each full circuit for making a personal record.
* It may be wise to place people from the same organization or department into different clusters of chairs.
* If numbers do not fit, facilitators can take part, or volunteers can sit out and observe, or an extra pair of chairs can be added to one or more circles (in which case stop the bigger circles when the smaller circles have finished their round).
* Write down the times when change-overs must take place. (Otherwise it is easy to mess up the timing.)

(With one Margolis wheel I noticed that one of the pairs was not talking. When I asked why, I was told: 'She just said, "use your own best judgement"'.)

Source: Participatory Learning and Action: A Trainer's Guide [see **21**:1, pp201–202] citing Alan Margolis, personal communication.

17 Commitments and follow-up

Commitments to follow-up can multiply the value of a workshop, training or course. They are not always appropriate. If commitments are to be made, allow enough time for them to be made properly.

COMMITMENTS

Commitments can be by groups or by individuals. Group commitments make sense where several people come from the same organization or area and can follow up together. Individual commitments make sense when participants will scatter.

Commitments can be verbal or written. Written ones demand more thought and provide a record. One good way is to invite participants to reflect and write on flip charts. These are then displayed, and each presents to the group in turn.

Tips and options

- Judge near the time whether inviting commitments will work. Sometimes the chemistry and/or the occasion are not right. Don't do it if people will think they are being got at.
- Ask all to start by reflecting on where they hope to have got to in, say, three or six months' time.
- Invite each to write a postcard to themselves with their commitments. The organizers mail these at a future date. (This idea comes from the International Workshop on Participatory Monitoring and Evaluation held in the Philippines in November 1998.)
- Encourage teams to form to discuss follow-up. They can be by geographical or administrative area, subject, organization or some other natural grouping.
- Encourage specifics – networking, alliances, further meetings – with dates and responsibilities.
- Report: discuss who will write and distribute a report or notes – purpose, form, contents, distribution and deadlines. (Short, sharp, timely and action-oriented notes are often better than fuller reports.)
- If all agree, include the follow-up commitments in any report. For an example see *The ABC of PRA* [see **21**:7, pp83–86]. I can testify that this has a powerful effect.

18 Moving but staying connected

Stand in a circle in a large open space. Ask everyone to look around and silently select two other people. Then everyone moves to form an equilateral, equal-sided triangle with the two selected. The effect can be remarkable, even wonderful, as all keep moving. When one moves, many others do too.

After a time, stop and invite reflections – staying in touch, how we are all connected, how we can affect one another at a distance, how our small actions affect larger systems...

This has been done with 15–350 people.

Source: Shaw and Patterson.

19 Logistics

Travel arrangements always deserve care. Worries can distract and disturb participants. Have a clearly identified person responsible. See that home travel arrangements are made well in advance. Give names, addresses, telephones, faxes, emails of all to all. (This is mundane, basic, very useful and easily overlooked.)

20 Ceremony and/or celebration and thanks

There may be diplomatic and courtesy reasons for a formal wind-up, but it is usually best avoided. Local VIPs may appreciate rather more being invited to:

A party! Hand over the stick. Encourage participants to organize any final event. A committee of volunteers can usually do this. Enjoy.

Thanks to those who have worked behind the scenes are easily forgotten and usually much appreciated.

And finally

21 Invent and improvise your own ways of ending

Part 3
Messing Up

8

21 Mistakes I Make in Workshops

I repeatedly mess up in workshops. Here are mistakes I have made, some of them again and again. And these are only the ones I am aware of and prepared to admit to. The tip of an iceberg?

There is a species called professional facilitator. These are people who have been trained as trainers and facilitators. They don't mess up. Or rather, they only mess up in a very professional way. I must be careful what I say. After all, they too are human. But they are a bit like psychiatrists. They know how to handle difficult situations, dissent and rebellion. I don't. They know how to focus a focus group. I don't. The only thing is, as with psychiatrists, their very professionalism can make them just a tiny bit less spontaneous, open, real. Not that I am spontaneous, open or real. Just amateur. So, if you too mess up and don't know what to do, join the club.

Boobs and bad habits are easier to list than to correct. It is also tempting to become complacent about them. And some are fun. Some of mine are serious, especially bad time management. But others I do not want to change. Which of these delinquencies would you want to hang on to?

Here we go:

1 Flapping before the start

Losing my cool, rushing around, misplacing things, taking it out on the convenors for the terrible room, immobile chairs, late arrival of slide projector, slide projector which mangles slides or shoots them into the air, archaic overhead projector, lack of an extension lead, screen that won't go up and then when up falls over, lack of wall space, squeaky chalk, useless boards, inadequate flip charts, round seeds that roll around all over, missing masking tape (I've put it down somewhere), curtains that don't black out, excessive heat or cold, noisy fans, roaring traffic ... and then failing to greet people as they come in, and starting in chaos.

FLAPPING

2 Spinning out the start

Taking too long with initial hiccups – preamble, introductions, jokes, asking about timings, checking out the programme, giving information about sources, documents and contacts ... so that the start on substance is late. (I have a deep insecurity – the fear of running out of things to fill the time later on. This is idiotically irrational as later on there has never been time enough.)

3 Putting down participation

Asking for views on the programme and then ignoring them. Sometimes I ask for a buzz on the programme, and suggestions. But rarely do any suggestions come. People do not know what the items on the programme really are, or what the options might be, so the consultation is a farce. Facipulation of a consensus, or rather acquiescence, based on ignorance. Worse, once, in Uppsala, I overruled a show of hands about something in a programme when it gave what I thought was the 'wrong' answer. Dreadful behaviour.

4 Messing with a microphone

Forgetting to use it, failing to switch it on, tripping over the cord, holding it too close or too far away, leaving it behind when walking around to show things, giving up and shouting without it...

5 Grotty gear

Using smeared and smudged overhead transparencies and terrible old torn wall charts (secretly proud because they have Russian subtitles from a training in Kyrgyzstan).

6 Muddling and missing things

Showing slides upside down. And 'I shall now illustrate this with a transparency'. But I can't find it. I know perfectly well that it is somewhere in the pile. It was there earlier. It is wilfully, malevolently, hiding. I mess about searching, more and more distracted, frantic, panicking, waffling fatuously to fill in, until finally, after all the damage has been done, I give up. 'Well, anyway, what it would have shown is...' (captured on video this was so ghastly I could not bring myself to watch it a second time).

MUDDLING

7 Presenting too much

Four or five slides only, but oh, yes, there are these others, and of course for this group I have to show... and it ends up as 20–30 (snores in the dark at the back of the room). Or too many overheads too fast with too much detail and not enough explanation or time to take the content in.

8 : 2–7   21 MISTAKES I MAKE IN WORKSHOPS

8 Not answering questions

Inviting questions on cards, clustering them, showing them on the wall, promising to deal with them, and then not doing so. (A dreadful case of this at Cornell.)

9 Monopolizing

Taking all the time for my presentations, sharings and exercises, and failing to make space for others to contribute and share.

10 Tolerating terrible talkers

Giving garrulous gasbags (usually male and over 50, but not, of course, including myself) too much time to talk, to the fury and frustration of others.

11 Getting rattled

Losing the plot, panicking, reacting defensively to questions, struggling to keep going when others' eyelids droop, longing for it to be over ...

12 Hypocritically prattling, pontificating, preaching

Talking top-down about participation, lecturing about not lecturing, preaching about not preaching.

13 Distracted and distracting behaviour

Manic impatience, waving arms, tearing hair.

14 Insensitivity

Being insensitive to culture or gender (asking Iranians to write the wrong 'first' name on their name tags; insisting that a senior woman should be a male lion (in 'Jungle'); telling an English in-joke about Winston Churchill to students from the South) or showing someone in a bad light (the worst near-disaster was when I was going to show a slide of a dominator, only to notice just in time that he was in the audience); putting up a big chart about domination immediately under a photograph of a country's less than democratic leader, and then instead of leaving it there, drawing attention by removing it (the chart, not the photo).

15 Not meeting people, rushing, being rude

Being busy and abrupt in between sessions, preoccupied with preparing for the next part of the programme, promising to talk later, and then listening and talking if at all with a distracted half attention while packing up in a panic to catch a train or plane. Taking down charts while a distinguished visitor is still talking (Lucknow).

16 Digressing

Adding in bits, indulging in anecdotes, going off at tangents, forgetting things to cover, flapping and then running out of time.

17 Squeezing the breaks

Truncating tea/coffee and lunch breaks, making them too short, and then fidgeting and complaining when participants do not return from them 'on time'.

18 Failing to finish off

Quite appalling. Almost always. Not just not answering questions that have been raised, but failing to tie it all together to make sense of the day, *leaving no time for reflection*, and forgetting to thank the organisers.

SQUEEZING THE BREAKS

19 Doing damage

Dropping a slide projector, using permanent markers on a whiteboard (nightmare), knocking over and bending a screen (why are they so awkward, with three legs that buckle and collapse, and a mast which once fully erect collapses catastrophically), and peeling off plaster to leave scarred walls when removing masking tape.

20 Leaving things behind

That chart someone was copying out. That video that was shown. That last slide in the projector. Those books used to prop up the front of the projector. And once a whole carousel (Manchester).

Mercifully, I have run out of numbers, because worst of all is *making this list complacently for fun* and to show off by place-dropping. All the same, making this list has jolted me over my bad time management. Perhaps I really will try to do something about that.

21 And what about you? Have you got 21?

9

21 Horrors in Participatory Workshops

MacPherson's principle (with other incarnations as Murphy's Law and Sod's Law, and qualified by O'Reilly's corollary – that MacPherson was an incorrigible optimist) is the law of cussedness, that if something can go wrong, it will go wrong. It is liable to manifest itself in participatory workshops. Certainly, something is always wrong or goes wrong. On top of that, as a facilitator one makes ghastly mistakes [see **8**].

It is not just during a workshop that things can go wrong. It is also before and after.

Before a workshop, organizers turn away keen and good uninvited people. They charge a fee that distresses and deters students, the unwaged, voluntary workers and others strapped for cash. This can be so sad. Numbers should not be a problem as long as there is space [see **13**]. University faculty seem especially prone to turf behaviour ('This is *our* workshop for *our* course') and saying no to people unless it is for an open lecture. I wonder why.

Then, after a workshop, a record or report of the workshop is promised by the organizers, but is never written, or written months later, or so long after that no one reads it. Or it is so inaccurate that it takes hours to correct, and then, after correction, a final version never comes.

In the workshop process itself, sometimes things being wrong or going wrong makes the best things happen. You are forced to improvise. Instead of showing slides, you demonstrate on the floor. Instead of making a presentation, you facilitate something more participatory. Disasters and difficulties are anyway for enjoying. The scope they offer for learning is generous. Treasure them. The worse they are, the better stories they will be for later.

Here are some horrors, mostly ones I have walked into. Forgive the shameless place-dropping.

1 A traffic jam holds you up on the way to the workshop. When you arrive already late to prepare the room, you find it locked. The janitor does not come for another 20 minutes... biting of nails and gnashing of teeth (Ahmedabad).

LOCKED OUT

2 You move all the chairs and tables the night before, to make the seating informal. Overnight, diligent janitors or conventional colleagues do their duty and restore the furniture to its formal default mode of schoolroom lines or a set hollow square. (This can happen anywhere but the risks are exceptionally high in South Asia.)

3 You arrive to find the seats fixed to the floor (Johannesburg, Mumbai) or tiered in a lecture theatre mode (Durban, London).

4 Some participants are getting a per diem and others not (in southern Africa this stalled an international workshop for 24 hours); or some participants (villagers in Shinyanga, Tanzania) are getting lower per diems than others they consider their peers.

5 A PAIN (Pompous And Insensitive Notable) opens the workshop. A high table on a dais has been diligently decorated with potted plants. The PAIN is male and ageing. Because he is an Important Person, participants have dressed formally. He is late. The organizers fidget and fret. When he finally arrives, everyone stands up. Disabled as he is by long experience of being listened to with proper, decent respect, he drones on and on about his personal experiences in a world long since past, and pet ideas which he has preserved unchanged for decades. Participants look surreptitiously, then openly, at their watches. The press has been invited. When the PAIN finally finishes his peroration, they ask irrelevant questions about local politics. Afterwards there is a prolonged tea break. Fawning supplicants flock to get their word in with the Big Man. When he leaves, half the morning has been lost. The furniture has to be rearranged. The participants have learnt nothing. The PAIN has learnt nothing. The wrong tone has been set. But protocol has been observed (this can happen almost anywhere).

6 It is stiflingly hot from central heating (a basement in Denmark in winter) or shiveringly cold with no heating (a hotel in Kunming, China, in winter, with snow falling outside).

7 Fans and/or air-conditioning make you inaudible (India), or roaring traffic drowns you out (India), a shipbuilding warehouse echoes fortissimo (Copenhagen), or a supercilious swan stares down at you through the window (Amsterdam).

8 A microphone is needed and is fixed so that you cannot walk about, and when you do, people cannot hear you; or it is on a cord that you trip over, pulling out the plug and inflicting minor abrasions (Band-aid is rarely on the kit list for workshops); or it throws tantrums with an excruciating cacophony of squeaks which cannot be silenced (global phenomenon).

9 The slide projector is the wrong sort, or rotates the carousel without stopping, or has slots too narrow to take your fatter slides, or jams and mangles your precious cardboard-mounted ones (IDS, Sussex, UK), or throws them explosively into the air (catch them if you can) (London, Brighton); or will not focus, or will only focus with a tiny picture; or you negligently drop and dent the projector which is never the same again, and the British Council who lent it are not amused (Dhaka); or the windows will not darken or black out (Karachi).

10 The only plug is far from the screen, and there is no extension lead (about one workshop in four) (Jethro Pettit carries his own).

11 The electricity goes off when you were going to use, or were using, a slide projector or overhead projector (India, especially Bihar where wags call the time when the electric current actually does come 'breakdown'). 'Well, what the next picture would have shown...'

A PLUG TOO FAR

12 The video cannot be made to work (mainly countries in the North), or your television systems are not compatible (North America); or when the video does play the picture flips continuously up the screen, or shivers uncontrollably, or decorates itself with vibrating, horizontal lines; or the soundtrack is garbled, or crackles and booms; or your cassette has the Russian soundtrack and no one knows Russian.

13 Masking tape unpeels from the walls and wall charts distract as they fall down noisily (Johannesburg); or on removal it plucks plaster from the walls leaving permanent pock marks (suggesting low construction specifications or poor supervision of contractors), which does not contribute to love and harmony with the workshop's hosts (IDS, Sussex, in the past; World Bank, Delhi).

14 The pile on the carpet is so thick that paper cannot be laid flat and beans for matrix scoring roll all over and off the paper (IMF, Washington).

15 Someone knows the answer to a teaser and gets it at once, destroying your plan to show how hard it is to guess poor people's realities (and also depriving you of the money you have wagered to make it more interesting) (Lucknow, Delhi, Helsinki, Brighton ...).

16 A self-confident saboteur (usually a professional facilitator and highly trained trainer) criticizes the conduct of the workshop and suggests a radical change of programme; or reflects in plenary not on what was learnt from an exercise but on how patronizingly simplistic it was (Denmark, not a Dane!).

17 The pens have dried out and leave only faint smudges on the flip chart (all over the place).

18 Powers that be prevail. Just before starting you are ordered to replace batiks you have unscrewed from the wall to make space for wall charts (never mind where); practicals with chalk are sabotaged by janitors or police: 'You can't do that there 'ere' (DFID in London); or you are ordered out before you have finished, early on a Friday evening (endemic in England).

DRY PENS

19 The kind people who take down the wall charts at the end leave on the strips of masking tape. When you unroll them the next time, the charts rip to pieces (all over the place).

20 The next day you discover you have lost your final transparency: you left it on the overhead projector. You cannot find the slide you ended with: you left it in the slide projector. And you cannot trace some bulky papers you had with you: you used them to prop up the front of the slide projector (common enough but I forget where).

21 Collect and treasure your own catastrophes. Share them. Enjoy.

10

21 Ways to Not Answer a Question

This was inspired by Miles Kington, in the *Independent* (London) 12 January 1998. He listed ten phrases that indicate that somebody is about to evade a question they have just been asked. Some of those that follow come from Kington.

When asked a difficult question, you may feel:

WHEN ASKED A DIFFICULT QUESTION

- I'm sunk
- This is the end
- Death, where is thy sting?

You may be tempted to respond with a flat refusal to respond, like:

- 'That takes us outside our subject'

or

- 'We can either cover the subject, or I can take questions, but we can't do both'

I do not recommend either. It is safer to conceal your real feelings. Try this two-stage approach.

STAGE 1: FLATTER

This buys time for you to think and select for Stage 2. Disarm and deflect the questioner with flattery. Start with one of these ten:

- '*Good* question!'
- 'Well asked!'
- 'Congratulations!'
- 'That's absolutely the right one to ask.'
- 'That's spot on.'
- 'I was hoping someone would bring this up.'
- 'That is a truly *searching* question.'
- 'Not everyone thinks to ask that.'
- 'I was not expecting anyone to ask such a *key* question.'

- 'I can see that someone is really thinking.'
- 'That's the 64,000 dollar one. Take the jackpot.'

Alternatives to *good*, *searching* and *key* include:

Acute, advanced, astute, basic, bright, brilliant, cardinal, central, challenging, creative, critical, crucial, dazzling, deep, discerning, enlightened, essential, excellent, far-sighted, fine, first-rate, formative, forward-looking, frontier, fundamental, illuminating, important, insightful, inspirational, inspiring, instructive, intelligent, intriguing, keen, knowing, original, penetrating, perceptive, pivotal, profound, seminal, sharp, shrewd, significant, smart, stunning, super, superb, thoughtful, trail-blazing, visionary, vital, well-informed, wise, wonderful ... and with some acute and ... wonderful creativity (or with a dictionary of synonyms) you will be able to add more in English, or (with your own knowledge or other dictionaries) in other languages. Or you can simply say: 'That is, of course, *the* question'.

Then you can proceed to:

STAGE 2: EVADE

- **'I don't know.'**

Disarming, but only use once. Keep in reserve if you can.

- **'If we knew the answer to that, we wouldn't be here.'**

- **'There is no one answer to that.'**

- **'Can anyone help us with this one?'**

- **'We mustn't rush into trying to answer that.'**

- **'Good. Could someone write that up so that we don't forget it?'**

- **'We will be coming to that later.'**

- **'How would you answer that yourself?'**

- **'In answering that, each of us has to use our own best judgement.'**

- **'I think you will find that answers to that question will emerge in our later sessions.'**

- 'We need our collective wisdom for this one. Let's have a buzz.'

- 'The best person to answer that is … (an absent colleague).'

- 'The book/article/journal to read on that is…'

- 'We have to ask ourselves what is the best way to set about seeking an answer to such an (*italicized adjective*) question.'

- 'Let me rephrase that…' (into a question you *can* handle).

- 'Remind me to come back to that in the last session.'

- 'Heavens – is that the time?'

- 'Gosh – isn't that a green woodpecker over there?'

- 'I see the coffee has arrived.'

- 'I am awfully sorry but I am having some trouble with …'

  Exit, embarrassed, displaying discomfort with a plausible part of the body and head for the toilet. Put off pursuers with 'Don't worry. I'll be perfectly all right. I need to deal with this on my own' in a strangled voice.

- **Invent and improvise to suit your own personal style.**

Part 4
Groups, Seating and Size

11

21 Ways of Forming Groups

Teachers, trainers and facilitators often need to form groups. Much good learning and discovery comes through group activities and discussions. So this 21 is a menu of methods for forming different sorts of groups. There are surely many, many more.

Two issues recur.

1   *Size of group.* Choice of size is a fascinating topic. There are many views and preferences. Mine keep on changing, but for the moment can be summarized as:

   •   pairs for instant short (10–100 seconds) buzzes, turning to neighbours;
   •   threes or at most fours for longer buzzes;
   •   pairs or at most threes for discussions and sharing that are personal and reflective, unless participants are very comfortable with each other and there is plenty of time, when up to say five or six can be all right;
   •   fours or at most fives for group work (eg PRA method practicals, brainstorm listing etc); even with five there is a tendency for one or two to be left out or marginalized;
   •   larger groups where only a few have relevant experience of the topic, or for sharing by one or a few peers, or where some participants would rather keep quiet [see **20**].

Note that when participants are left to form groups, they tend to be larger groups than requested. For example, if you say 'groups of four' there will usually be some fives, even sixes.

2   *Duration of group.* Some groups gel and work well. Others are tense, awkward and frustrating, especially when there are dominators. Listen, observe and judge whether to leave groups alone for more than one activity, or whether to reshuffle them.

   When asked in public whether they wish to stay together or reshuffle, some may be reluctant to opt for reshuffling for fear of offending others. One solution is to ask everyone to face you. First those wanting new groups close their eyes. Then those not wanting new groups close their eyes. This rapid secret vote will help you to see what best to do.

Reshuffling and mixing randomly or in various structured ways makes sense early in a workshop, to break the ice and widen contacts. Groups of longer duration often make sense later in a workshop and for fieldwork and its sequel.

Contents

The methods and groups can be classified as:

Random

1 By numbers
2 Number clumps
3 Circle and clump
4 Jungle
5 Picture jigsaw
6 Farmyard
7 Neighbours

Preset

8 Name plates or tags
9 Announce or display
10 Find and fit

Structured

11 Participatory
12 Team up
13 Diversity through numbering
14 Share the experts
15 Common interest groups

Self-selecting

16 Choose your own
17 À la carte

Sequenced

18 Coalesce or split
19 Send out, move on
20 Mixers
21 Improvise and invent

RANDOM

These are groups where participants are together entirely or largely by chance, and know that this is the case.

Uses

Random groups are good as mixers early in workshops. Forming them is usually quick, simple and fun. Most involve physical activity which wakes people up, and so leads in well to group discussions and other activities. Forming them is good also for the graveyard hour in the afternoon [see **6**].

1 By numbers

Easy, quick, transparent. Work out how many groups there will be for the group size you want. Ask people to number up to the number of groups needed, repeating until all have a number. So to form four random groups it goes 1, 2, 3, 4, 1, 2, 3, 4, 1, 2 …, etc. The 1s then form one group, the 2s another, and so on.

Tips

- Do the basic sums for group size before starting the counting!
- Seated groups can be jerkily slow in counting, uncertain who is next. Either let it sort itself out or help by pointing, or avoid the problem by doing it standing in a circle.
- Forming small groups in a large workshop can be lively; for example, 16 groups of three in a workshop of 48 people is noisily chaotic and groups have a sense of achievement when they finally find one another.

2 Number clumps

Very active and fun. Work out sets of numbers which add up to the number of participants. For example, with 15 participants it could be:

2 of 5, 1 of 2, 1 of 3 = 15

4 of 2, 1 of 3, 1 of 4 = 15

1 of 4, 1 of 5, 1 of 6 = 15

5 of 3   = 15

Shout out each set of sizes and numbers of groups in turn. Participants quickly try to form groups of those sizes. End with size and number of groups you want to form, in this case five groups of three.

Easy variant

Give numbers that do not necessarily add up. Then one or more people may be left out each time. But get the final number right.

3 Circle and clump

Energizing, interesting, fun, good social mixer, scope for inventions. Choose a personal characteristic with a sequence or gradation (examples below). Stand in a circle or straight line. Form groups by numbering (method 1 above), or simply say the required group size and leave it to edge-of-chaos self-organization with neighbours.

Examples of characteristics:

- Alphabetical order of first (or other) names. Active, fun, a good mixer for people on first meeting. People in groups can use and learn others' first names, and then have a collective first-name identity. Interesting groups may emerge, such as Muslim men under A.
- Birthday date or month, or sign of the zodiac. An opportunity for instant and intriguing group research on the seasonality of conception (dry season, Christmas, summer holidays, etc, according to conditions and culture). Identity by sign of the zodiac is a good icebreaker [see 5:10].
- Distance of home from place of workshop.
- Time it took to reach the workshop venue.
- Time of going to sleep the night before.
- Time it takes to get from home to work.

Tips

- Be careful with personal characteristics like age, height and weight if these are sensitive.
- Use for reflective self-ranking, for example, for talkativeness, ability to listen or dominance [see 18:4].

4 Jungle
(also known as fruit salad, vegetable stew, fish soup …)

Active, excellent energizer, and fun. Forms groups full of oxygen and adrenalin. Clears a central space free of chairs and impediments, usable for immediate group work.

All sit on chairs in a circle, with no empty chairs. You stand in the centre. Participants name wild animals (or fruits, vegetables, fish…) in sequence going round the circle, up to the number of groups desired. The names are then repeated in sequence (eg for three groups it might be 'lion, tiger, elephant, – lion, tiger, elephant, – lion …' etc). Check with hand raising that all know their animals.

JUNGLE

The person in the middle names an animal or animals. All those animals move and sit elsewhere. The person in the middle usually finds a seat easily. The new person in the middle names an animal or animals and finds somewhere to sit down. And so on.

When 'jungle' is shouted (or 'fruit salad', 'vegetable stew', or 'fish soup'…) everyone moves. When there has been enough activity, end up in the middle yourself, call a final jungle, and then ask participants to form their groups by animal (or fruit, vegetable, fish…).

Variant

Four is the normal upper limit for number of animals, fruits or vegetables but six or eight groups can be formed by having three or four jungle animals and then dividing the circle into one half females and the other half males. Check with hand-raising that all are clear about their animal and sex. (Normally everyone laughs, but do not pressurize as some may have deep blocks about changing sex.) Proceed with jungle. In addition to calling any animal and jungle, the person left in the centre can now also call 'all females' or 'all males'. At the end groups then form as female wolves, male wolves, female hyenas, etc, in emergent order from glorious and noisy chaos.

Tips

- Be sensitive to anyone who may have a disability.
- Spare chairs can be left in the centre and not used.
- For a structured mix in the otherwise random groups, ask like people to sit or stand together (eg for a mix of women and men, all women sit or stand together as do all men; for a mix of types of organization, those from each type of organization sit or stand together) or to line up graded by characteristic (eg by age for a mix of ages; amount of specialized experience for a mix of experience). They will then end up distributed through the groups.
- Insist that everyone must move.
- To add to the fun everyone can act or make the noise of their animal when moving.
- To increase activity, two animals can be named at the same time.
- If any animal is being left out, go in the centre yourself and name it.

5 Picture jigsaw

Fun, active and can give a humorous group identity. Cut up as many postcards or pictures as there are groups to be formed, with one piece for each member. Jumble these up. Participants are each given or asked to take one puzzle piece each, and then try to find their counterparts to make the picture. The group can take its name from the picture.

Tip

Choose cards or pictures with interesting identities.

6 Farmyard

Fun, active, and each group gains an animal identity. Decide the number of people you want in each group. Write animal names on slips of paper, each animal to be a group. Jumble up the slips. Hand them out or ask participants to pick them up. Ask them to act out their animals, both non-verbally and with animal noises, until they find each other.

Variant

Appoint a hunter/shepherd for each animal. Brief them outside the room. They then find their animals and gather them together.

7 Neighbours

Instant with pairs and quick with threes. Good for buzzes. Not fully random. Ask participants to discuss with their neighbours, one-to-one, or in groups of three, or if at tables, others at their table.

Tip

Avoid the Wimbledon syndrome (middle person's head moving from side to side to see and talk to neighbours). Suggest they move chairs so that they face one another, with an equilateral triangle for threes.

NEIGHBOURS

PRESET

These are groups where the composition of each group is wholly or largely determined by the facilitators in advance. Pre-allocated groups are useful where group composition and chemistry matter, where there are some difficult group members, and/or the groups will have to work together as teams over an extended period, for example, in fieldwork. Pre-allocation can assure an appropriate mix of disciplines, genders, experience, personality, local knowledge and language. But it can also lead to resentment and requests to change groups.

Tips

- To work out the composition of the groups or teams, write names on cards and sort on the ground or a table. Coloured marks can indicate characteristics that need to be matched or mixed (eg gender, organization, experience, language). This makes sorting and arranging quicker and easier.
- Use a searching and bonding game to bring the teams together (see 9 and 10 below). This reduces the chances of difficult negotiations to change groups.

8 Name plates or tags

For starting a workshop or a session. Names are either on name plates on tables, or table numbers or letters are written on the back of name tags that participants receive. Participants often welcome this as it relieves them of the decision of where and with whom to sit and can help them to mix with people they might not otherwise meet.

9 Announce or display

For forming teams or groups. Names and groups are handed out, read out or posted up. This is the most obvious, easy and common method. This can work well when time is short, groups will not meet for more than an hour or two, and all groups have the same task. Participants can welcome not having to decide for themselves, time is saved and no one is being deprived of a subject. (Used with full acceptance and good effect at a one-day workshop at Durham University in 1998.)

This can, though, provoke problems when forming longer-term groups or teams. People scrutinize the lists, wonder what criteria were used, see if they would rather be in another group, and quite often ask to change. To refuse change can be difficult, and be branded as non-participatory. To allow change can upset a careful balance.

10 Find and fit

Participatory, fun and tends to bond groups from the start. Cut up postcards or make jigsaws. Write members' names on the blank side of each piece. Hand out the pieces randomly. Each seeks the person whose name is on their piece and hands it over. Then all look for others with pieces that fit theirs. They come together then unselfconsciously with a sense of fun and achievement, having solved their first problem.

FIND AND FIT

The picture on the card gives the group its identity. Cards of wild animals serve well – elephant, lion, tiger, zebra, hippo, monkey, giraffe...

Tip

Carry with you a stock of animal postcards and a pair of scissors.

STRUCTURED

These are groups that contain a deliberate mix, specifying sorts of people to be in each group but not individually who those people should be.

Uses:

Mixed groups can ensure a range of points of view, and are more participatory than preset groups. They are useful for learning the points of views, knowledge, experience and skills of people from other backgrounds. The knowledge that people who are strangers, junior, young, female, etc, have been deliberately mixed can add to their voice and others' listening, especially if stated at the start as a reason for the grouping.

11 Participatory

A participatory approach needs sensitive facilitation. Done well with open and flexible participants it can lead to good ownership and consensus. Ask participants to brainstorm the criteria and categories for diversity in the groups (male–female, with and without a particular language, etc). List those in each category to see how many of them there can or should be in each group. Facilitate volunteering and allocation from the categories to the groups.

Options

1   A participant writes names on cards. These can be colour-coded for category of person. These are then stuck on a board as the groups are formed. Since all can see, suggestions can be made and people can volunteer or negotiate changes of groups to get the right mix.
2   Groups are formed physically in different parts of the room. Once started, others choose where to join, category by category, in appropriate numbers.

Sources: Somesh Kumar and Antonella Mancini

12 Team up

A participatory way to give the same desired mix of types of participants in each group. Good when groups should include two or three types.

This can be used to achieve a similar mix in each group by, for example, gender, junior–senior, discipline or profession, experience, fluency and comprehension of the language being used, or members of different courses.

Ask similar people to stand together. Then ask them to divide into smaller groups or even single people, depending on the numbers needed. They then find and bond with others. For example, to form mixed gender groups of five from 12 women and 18 men, the women form pairs and the men threes which then form six groups of five. This also works with numbers that are not exactly divisible.

Variant

Simply say what the composition of the groups should be and let order emerge from the edge of chaos.

13 Diversity through numbering

Straightforward, quick, slightly imprecise. Stand or sit by type, and then number as in 1 above, each type group in turn. When the number groups form they have a diverse mix.

Sometimes people sit in clusters – senior people in front, women behind, geographers all together (why?). In such cases, numbering without movement will also produce a diverse mix.

Numbering is also good for reshuffling. If groups have already formed, and then numbering takes place group by group, the new groups will be well mixed. For example, suppose there are already six groups of five. Numbering from one to five, group by group, will produce five new groups in which all members are new to each other, and can also represent all the discussion and learning that has taken place in the earlier groups.

14 Share the experts

To achieve a distribution of expertise to each group. Ask those with special knowledge, experience or skill to raise their hands. These may be, for example, people who have facilitated participatory mapping, done a cost-benefit analysis, or used participatory monitoring and evaluation. Others then cluster round them so that each group has one or more expert to share experience.

SHARE THE EXPERTS

15 Common interest groups

Useful for specialized discussion or considering a group position. Common interest groups bring together people who are similar in, for example, occupation, type of organization, country or region of origin or experience, age, seniority, gender, profession, or topic interest in, for example, health, agriculture or credit.

Tips

*   Common interest groups can be a stage in analysis or negotiation, followed by intergroup presentations and discussions.
*   Common interest groups are often useful towards the end of workshops to work out implications and action.

SELF-SELECTING

Participants select which group to join.

16 Choose your own [see **14**:17]

Good for commitment, ownership, adding to the agenda, giving space for leadership, enthusiasm and choice. Participants think of topics they wish to work on. Those with ideas announce them and seek recruits. Others choose which group to join.

Tips

*   If any important topic is missed or undersubscribed, raise the point for discussion.
*   If there is demand, there can be two or more rounds, so that each person can go to two or three topic groups.

17 À la carte

Participants choose from a preset menu. There are several ways of doing this:

1   List the topics for groups on flip charts. Participants sign up.
2   Ask for hands to be raised, topic by topic.
3   Post up topics in different places. Participants walk over to the topic of their choice.

Listing on a flip chart gives more time for reflection and trying to get into a group with friends or certain others. A little surprisingly, hand-raising can have advantages of:

* Speed.
* Ease of adjustment. If there are too many in one group, or too few in another, switches can be invited and encouraged without delay. This is harder to do when people have committed by writing up their names.
* Reduced effects from seeing who has already signed up.
* Fewer second thoughts as to whether it is the right group. However, those who raise hands tend to be more fickle and liable to change their minds.

Tip

If too many opt for a group, split it into two or more. Do this quickly before the group meets and gets going.

SEQUENCED

Many combinations and sequences are possible. They can be improvised on the spot.

18 Coalesce or split

A varied repertoire for active participation.

Examples

* Individuals reflect and make notes, and then share in small groups.
* After a group exercise in pairs or threes, these amalgamate into fours or sixes to share experience [see **18**:2–3].
* Divide large groups to discuss a subtopic, and then bring them together again.

Tip

The key is often to observe group dynamics and to take appropriate action.

19 Send out, move on

An easy and versatile enlivener and mixer, strangely underused. Ask each group to choose and send out someone. Those sent out either form their own new group or join another existing group or become observers.

Four main purposes can variously be served:

1   *Therapeutic.* Send out:
    • the person who talks or dominates most [see **19**:7];
    • the most senior;
    • the oldest;

    who may then become more aware of their behaviour and how they are perceived. If big talkers form a group, they neutralize each other. If quiet people form a group, they should find it easier to talk.

2   *Sharing.* Send out:
    • a messenger who will convey what has been discussed so that other groups can compare and learn;
    • those with special experience which they then pass on to the next group.

3   *Churning.* Send out:
    • whoever is tallest or shortest, has the longest or shortest hair, the biggest or smallest moustache, or some other unserious characteristic;
    • whoever would like to move;

    which is fun to liven things up.

4   *Observation, feedback, reporting...*
    Those moving on are given special roles, for example, when big talkers observe and map the interactions of those left in their groups and feedback what they notice [see **19**:14].

Tips

• Be wary: moving on can disturb and annoy a group that is doing well and is at ease with itself. Not every group always wants to lose its biggest talker or expert!
• Second, third and more rounds of movement can be made. (The Margolis wheel [see **7**:16] is a special case of move on in another sort of group).

20 Mixers

Excellent for combinations and sequences of analysis and sharing between disciplines or groups of people with special knowledge [**16**:9]. Rounds can alternate between groups with common knowledge, interest or expertise, and groups which share between these. If As have common knowledge with other As, Bs with Bs and so on, varied sequences and combinations are feasible. Numbers typically vary. Sorts of mixes include:

Like with like

AAAAA BBB CCCCCC DDD

Partial mixes

AAAB AABB CCCD CCCDD
ACC AACC AACC BBD BDD, etc

Maximum diversity

AABCCD AABCCD ABCCD

Tips
- Find a better way than this to explain the system.
- If there is a sequence of rounds, make sure that all know what they are going to share in subsequent rounds.

21 Improvise and invent your own

21 Arrangements for Seating

A blind spot?

As a subject, seating arrangements are strangely neglected. The manual *Participatory Learning and Action: A Trainer's Guide* [see **21**:1, pp15–17] identifies six main types:

1   rows of tables and chairs (like a classroom)
2   hollow U
3   fishbone or banquet style
4   conference table
5   circle or semi-circle of chairs
6   table trios

For its part, *VIPP: Visualisation in Participatory Programmes* [see **21**:14, pp 61–64] has quite precise instructions for four seating arrangements for chairs in relation to pin boards.

These two sources are exceptional. Most manuals or guides ignore the subject. Seating goes by default. Yet how we sit (or for that matter stand, squat, kneel or lie) affects how we feel and how we interact. Seating arrangements carry coded messages about relationships. They put us in positions ranged between disciplined and chaotic, formal and informal, centralized and decentralized, hierarchical and egalitarian, exposed and private, and threatening and non-threatening.

Institutionalized seating: fixed and default modes

Sometimes a seating arrangement is fixed. It is built into the architecture, as with tiered lecture theatres and auditoria (see 1 below). Or it is a function of the furniture like the long boardroom table (see 2 below) (how did they get it in through the door, or did they build the building around it?). Or it may be a side-effect of technology as with tables tethered by tangles of microphone wires.

More often though, when indoors, there are tables and chairs that are moveable, permitting flexible and varied arrangements. To an astonishing degree, though, teaching and training institutions have a default mode. Whatever may be done during a workshop, at the end everything is – has to be – 'put back in order'.

Default modes tell us about institutional cultures of teaching and learning. They also express and reinforce rituals of interaction.

Alas, they vary little. The most common is still classroom style (type 3 below), with rows of chairs and desks facing the 'teacher' or 'lecturer'. This is embedded in most of our psyches from the days when we were taught in school or lectured at in college.

Another arrangement, common in tertiary education and training institutes, is sitting in a seminar square or around a table. In the Institute of Development Studies at the University of Sussex (where I used to work and now enjoy myself), the default mode is a hollow square of tables (type 4 below). This is so entrenched that when new tables were ordered the shape was embodied in more durable form with special rounded pieces fixed at the four corners. These corner pieces are a bruising nightmare to unfix and refix, and, unlike tables, take up space uselessly when detached. On the positive side this provides an opportunity for teachers to become learners, taught by the porters who know how to dismantle and reassemble the corners. On the negative side it discourages participatory seating and approaches, makes it less likely that users will put the tables back together and makes more work for the default-mode restorers (the porters), who then have all the bother of putting them back themselves. All this encourages passive acceptance of the status quo and discourages many of the participatory approaches outlined in these 21s. Formality and hierarchy are then sustained, and participatory learning impeded.

In contrast, the default mode in NGO training institutions in South Asia is often egalitarian and levelling, either with no furniture and sitting on the floor, or with chairs around the edges of the room or in a circle.

Options

Choices almost always precede a workshop. Try to ensure a suitable room and furniture in advance. Whether you are successful or not, choosing how to arrange things can be stressful, but turn this on its head and make it fun. If you can, see the room or the place for the workshop well before it starts.

If the furniture is fixed, the options are:

- Accept it. Ugh. But move around and use other spaces.
- Unscrew it and move it. Normally unacceptable. Inadvisable if you want to be invited back.
- Accept for the start, then shift elsewhere.
- Find another place from the beginning. Often feasible, but you may have to be firm.

If the furniture is not fixed, the more obvious options fall into four groups according to whether you have:

	Chairs	Tables	
A	Yes	Yes	Normal
B	Yes	No	Less common, but can usually be arranged
C	No	Yes	Rare
D	No	No	Quite common in South Asia. Also out-of-doors

C is found in ActionAid Nepal with a long low table in a long room. Participants sit on the floor and can usually lean back against the wall. This is the pattern in at least three of their offices.

D can be brilliant for those able to sit in the lotus position, and less comfortable for others. Care is needed with those who have back problems, bony bottoms, arthritis or other disabilities. It helps to have something to lean back against. Lying is something else. In my view, few good interactions (I refer to those of a strictly professional nature) take place lying on the ground. For serious discussions it is better to sit up.

Most of the 21 that follow illustrate alternatives with A and B when the furniture is movable.

Pros and cons

Preferred patterns of seating vary: by facilitator; by participant; by purpose; by type of activity; by institutional tradition; and by more general culture. Matrix scoring of different arrangements by Faculty at the National Institute of Rural Development, Hyderabad, India, generated different criteria and different scores. Views can even differ about whether a feature is positive or negative.

Eye contact is an example. Usually this is taken as good. Eye contact is high with egalitarian seating like an empty square of tables or chairs in a circle. But it can inhibit. The speaker is aware of many people. It can be bad for those who are shy to speak. In contrast, with muddled up seating, as after a buzz in threes, there is little eye contact and less awareness of others. I have noticed a tendency in such muddled up plenaries for quiet conversations to replace more assertive speeches, for remarks to be shorter and more interactive, for some who were silent to speak, and for contributions to be more reflective.

Some questions to ask:

- *Objectives:* what do you want to achieve with the seating? How centred, decentred, flexible?
- *Sequences:* do you want to plan these (eg moving from formal to informal)?
- *Acoustics:* how easily will everyone be able to hear you, and each other?
- *Visibility:* will any screen, posters, slides, flip chart stands be visible to everyone?
- *Buzz groups:* how easy will it be to break into these?
- *Tables, side tables, just chairs, or no chairs:* do people need a surface for writing, or can that be dispensed with?[1]
- *Comfort:* will participants be physically comfortable?
- *Space:* how well can space be used, especially if a room is crowded and cramped?

---

1 At the time of discussing whether to have tables for writing on or not, consider whether there will be time for recollection, reflection and recording [see **16**:19]. If there will be such time, participants can be told and asked to remember, through the session(s) what they are going to want to write down later. This will tend to reinforce memorizing, which note taking often postpones forever.

- *Talkers and the timid:* will dominators find it easy to dominate? Will the timid talk?
- *Cow-uncompliant:*[2] will participants mix and sit in different places, if that is desirable?

Sequences

Sequences of different seating arrangements can be needed and can help. Sometimes there has to be a formal start, with the paraphernalia of Guest-of-Honour, Keynote Speaker, and jolly polite tea, coffee and biscuits afterwards. That may require school assembly seating. But after that, arrangements of increasing informality can be used. Many workshops go through such sequences of seating, often towards a circle of chairs and an open space in the middle, or a muddled jumble.

One sequence I used for a few years was:

1   table threes (see 9 below);
2   amalgamate to groups of six, putting two tables together;
3   move tables to walls and form a circle of chairs for 'Jungle' [see **11**:4] to form groups;
4   use the central space for group work on the ground.

Another good one is to start with chairs in several concentric U-shapes (necessary if numbers are high), and then muddle them up for buzzes. DSD (decentred seating disorder) is not a pathological condition of the backside but an informal and friendly arrangement of chairs.

Tips

- Arrange seating and tables in advance. Ask for help. Be there when it is done. Enjoy the physical exercise.
- Be daring. Try new arrangements.
- Think through sequences to vary the seating.
- Anticipate changes you want and ask participants to help make them.
- Decentre for democratic participation. Go away from the board or screen. Move around. Sit mixed up with others. Success is sometimes best achieved when people are not looking at you and not addressing you, and good conversations take off.

---

2 The allusion is to the tendency, well known to farmers, for cows to return to the same stall. This phenomenon may be common to many mammals. Old people in homes have 'my seat', and some participants in workshops do the same, even when 'their' seat is not labelled. Interestingly, this seems often to be more in the minds of others than of the putative occupants. 'Oh, sorry, is this your seat?' There can also be a temporal dimension to rights to a seat. Gordon Conway recounts his experience on a train from Patna to Delhi. Finding someone in the seat for which he had a booking he was met with 'Yes Sir, this is indeed your seat, *but this is yesterday's train.*'

A last word can be these questions:

- Are you using the same seating all through a workshop or course? If so, is something wrong?
- Are you using the same seating, in the same sequence, as you were three years ago? If so, is something wrong?
- Do you think you have got it right, for all time? If so, have you become a fossil and is it time to retire?

Contents

Immovable

1 Lecture theatre and amphitheatre
2 Boardroom table and racecourse

With movable chairs and tables

3 Classroom and angled classroom
4 Hollow square and hollow U
5 Double U
6 Fishbone
7 Banquet
8 Equilateral trios
9 Table threes

Chairs without tables

10 School assembly
11 Half circles and Us
12 Circles and open clams, single and double

13 Group with facilitator
14 Buzzing clusters (with various numbers)
15 SOSOTEC
16 Fishbowl
17 The Margolis wheel

Without chairs or tables

18 Democratic on the ground ('doing something')
19 Sitting against the wall
20 Walking and standing
21 Invent, experiment and improvise your own

IMMOVABLE

1 Lecture theatre and amphitheatre

These appear to be formal traps, limited to lecturing and question and answer. But buzzes are possible (see Tip) and there is often good space outside for other activities.

LECTURE THEATRE

Tip

- For buzzes ask those in odd rows to turn around, stand or kneel on their seats, and talk to those behind them. After a pause of disbelief, the effect can be electrifying [see **17**:20].

AMPHITHEATRE   ODD-ROWS-RISE

2 Boardroom table and racecourse

Cow-compliance and other nightmares prevail

These are among the worst patterns for participatory work, or even for formal presentations. By the end of the day, if not earlier, participants (I am inclined to call them victims) may be in one of two conditions: either they have given up, or they have a crick in the neck. Even if the group is small, conversations of more than pairs are virtually impossible between those sitting on the same side. Also anyone presenting from one end can be intimidated by two lines of heads in enfilade craning to face them.

BOARDROOM

The National Institute of Rural Development at Hyderabad, India, is of special interest here. Under a succession of directors-general, all from the Indian Administrative Service, it has expanded. New buildings have been planned and put up. The inclination or reflex has been to build not new training buildings, but a new administration block.

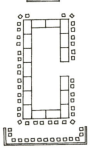

RACECOURSE

So a succession of old administration blocks has been handed on, or rather down, to training. The heritage bequeathed includes long thin rooms for hierarchical meetings. Some of these rooms are occupied by long oval boardroom tables. Others have been colonized in similar pattern by elongated racecourses of tables tied down by microphone wires. In these ways, the hierarchical spatial relationships of administration have been passed on to be perpetuated in training.

Tips

- When faced with boardrooms or racecourses protest with a fitting mix of politeness and passion.
- Counter cow-compliance and neck cricks by swapping seats and sides.
- Contrive buzzes of threes by asking every third person to move their seat back.

WITH MOVABLE CHAIRS AND TABLES

3 Classroom and angled classroom

Formal though these are, they allow some freedom of movement and can be rearranged.
The angled classroom gives more contact between participants, and some scope for buzzes, though for buzzing the seating is bad for those at the ends who are far apart.

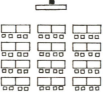 

CLASSROOM

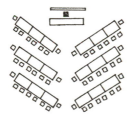 

ANGLED CLASSROOM

4 Hollow square and hollow U

These arrangements expose participants to much eye contact with others at a distance, with the formality of tables intervening. This inhibits some, and accentuates the tendency to rehearse what one wants to say rather than listen to others and react. Speeches are more common than conversations.

The apparent symmetry of the hollow square is misleading: for example, those next to a presenter or facilitator are both exposed (by being at 'head table') and marginalized by the difficulty of catching the presenter's or facilitator's eye, and having to turn round to see the screen or board. Another disadvantage is that the centre space is difficult to enter or use.

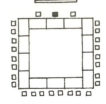

HOLLOW SQUARE

The hollow U is closer to the classroom, and the presenter or facilitator is more dominant. But easier access to the centre space can be useful for activities.

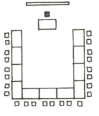

HOLLOW U

5 Double U

The double U enhances the dominance of the presenter or facilitator. On the positive side, it fits more people into a space than the hollow U, and reduces the ratio of eye contact to numbers of participants. It can be fixed or flexible. It is a favourite in offices and training centres with square rooms and pressure on space.

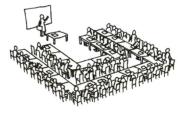

DOUBLE U

6 Fishbone

The fishbone is like the angled classroom with the tables rotated through 90 degrees. It is more participatory and table- and group-centred: hardly any of the seats faces the head of the room. Most, to face that way, have to turn their seats round and some then have no table barrier in front of them. The table itself, and group discussions at the table, are an easy mode of interaction.

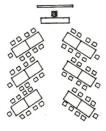

FISHBONE

7 Banquet

Banquet seating centres even more on the tables (often pairs of tables put together) for group discussions. It is a good form for small participatory workshops and conferences. It allows for decentred cross conversations between people at the different tables better than the

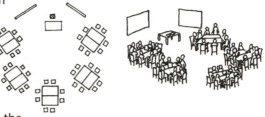

BANQUET

fishbone, and can leave a useful centre space (unless another banquet table is put there).

A more participatory and even less hierarchical variant is to have the tables in a circle with equal status and no 'head table'. Sitting in seats which face the central space makes conversations easy and presentations can easily be made from any point.

8 Equilateral trios

The egalitarian symmetry of this arrangement is slightly offset by its angularity. But it can work well.

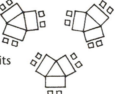

EQUILATERAL 3S

9 Table threes

This improbable seating is worth considering, at least as a stage in a sequence. The threes are good for buzzes. The angle of the table, pointing to the head, with the three sitting at one end, puts their heads close together. Tables can easily be amalgamated to make sixes.

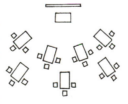

TABLE 3S

CHAIRS WITHOUT TABLES

10 School assembly

The chairs are normally moveable. For all its formality, a scraping of chairs on floor can transform this in the twinkling of an eye into many small discussions.

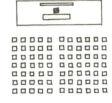

SCHOOL ASSEMBLY

Tip

• If the chairs are moveable and all occupied, you can change quickly to radically different patterns in different locations by asking each to pick up and carry the chair they are sitting on.

11 Half circles and Us

These are favoured in VIPP. The screen or flip chart is visible to all. The presenter/facilitator is well placed to control, show and facilitate. There is good flexibility for moving to other seating arrangements, and a convenient central space.

HALF CIRCLE U

12 Circles and open clams, single and double

Single circles are widely adopted as democratic and participatory. The symmetry of the seating is obvious. All the same, they can intimidate, especially when there are large numbers. Shy people can feel exposed. The facilitator can still dominate.

CIRCLE

Surprisingly, open clams, with two arcs of chairs facing each other, seem to be more democratic. Each seat has an opposite seat. No seat can command as much attention as in a circle. With larger numbers, too, open clams also have the advantage of allowing entry at both ends. They entail slightly less sense of personal exposure. There is great freedom of movement.

OPEN CLAM

12 : 10–12 21 ARRANGEMENTS FOR SEATING

Double circles and double open clams have further advantages. The eye contact to numbers ratio is lower, and any sense of exposure less. No one person can be seen by all the others. The facilitator is less dominant. Voices can come from many directions. In these respects,

DOUBLE CIRCLE

double circles and double clams are more empowering and more democratic, for any given number of participants, than single circles or single clams.

13 Group with facilitator

The facilitator initiates discussion and then gradually withdraws as others talk to each other. This is a classic pattern for a focus group. The gradual and crucial shift is from members of the group listening to, looking at and talking to the

CIRCLE OBSERVER REMOVE

facilitator to them listening to, looking at and talking to each other.

14 Buzzing clusters (with various numbers)

Many patterns are possible. As facilitator, you can decentre yourself. Plenary conversations can follow buzzes. Low eye contact makes the context friendly to shy talkers.

BUZZ CLUSTERS

Tip

* Forming buzzes, recommend lifting and turning round chairs so that all face each other, for example, for a three as an equilateral triangle.

15 SOSOTEC

[See **14**:16–20]. A variety of self-forming activities take place in different parts of the room and even outside it. The diagram illustrates the informality and diversity of SOSOTEC. It should not be taken as a model.

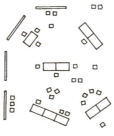

SOSOTEC

16 Fishbowl

In fishbowl seating an activity takes place in the centre of a circle or clam (or double circle or double clam). All can observe and hear. This is excellent for debates or discussions between those in the middle.

FISHBOWL

17 The Margolis wheel

The essence is pairs of chairs facing each other, arranged like a wheel. Those in the outer circle rotate after brief (usually three to four minute) consultations or exchanges with those in the centre. [See **7**:16].

MARGOLIS WHEEL

WITHOUT CHAIRS OR TABLES

18 Democratic on the ground ('doing something')

Discussions and analytical activities on the ground have a democratic character, tending to weaken, equalize or reverse power relationships [see **14**:16 and **19**:17].

In discussions, it is harder for any one person to be important and dominate unless they stand up. Power relationships may be subtly weakened. Those who can sit cross-legged comfortably (often those who are younger and/or from countries in the South) have more eye contact and are more at ease than those who cannot (often those who are older and/or from countries in the North).

USE THE GROUND

In analytical activities like diagramming and card sorting, the democracy of the ground is yet more marked. There is less eye contact than when sitting in chairs or at a table. Those who are more senior or important tend to be marginalized if they remain standing. Conversely, those who are more junior and less important tend to get down on the ground and take over. Actions in drawing, diagramming or moving cards can be made without words or with minimal words and without eye contact. Several people can take part simultaneously without any individual in control as part of a self-organizing system [see **14**:16].

Tips

- Be sensitive to disability. Some people cannot, or cannot easily, get down on the ground.

- Precede work on the ground with an energizer.
- Be cautious about outdoor discussions lying on grass in hot weather. Participatory and politically correct though they appear, they are sometimes less effective than sitting round a table on chairs.

19 Sitting against the wall

This is common in South Asia. Those with stiff limbs find this more comfortable than sitting unsupported. It is easier for those who cannot manage the lotus position to take notes when there is something to lean against. Any facilitator tends to be less dominant than when chairs are used.

SITTING AGAINST THE WALL

20 Walking and standing

Horses can sleep while standing but rarely humans. Standing and walking around to look at posters and charts is a good non-seating wake-up activity to mix in with others. Using wall charts, or flip charts in different parts of a room, it is a great way to break up a session, especially in the afternoon graveyard.

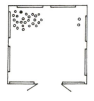

WALKING AND STANDING

Tips

- Anticipate by placing flip charts or posters strategically anywhere except in the 'front' of the room.
- Ensure that the visuals are visible by putting them high enough.
- Where necessary, encourage people in front to sit down. Otherwise those at the back may drift away.

21 Invent, experiment and improvise your own

21 Ideas for Participatory Workshops with Large Numbers

Participatory workshops can be for any number, up to 200 or perhaps even more. Those considered 'large' here are with around 30 or more people. The largest I have known began with 180 (in Chiang Mai in Thailand) but half left after a time, I was told, because of language and acoustics. Paradoxically, large workshops are often easier to manage than small ones. With size can come animation, noise, movement and a certain freedom for participants: safe anonymity to shelter the shy, space to grumble for the disgruntled and cover to slip away for the bored. The challenges for facilitators are also a special sort of fun.

Large workshops tend to be short. The ideas that follow are based mainly on experience with day-long workshops concerned with development topics like poverty and health, seasonality, and participatory approaches, behaviours and attitudes. They should work with any similarly short workshops with large numbers. Some tips are cross-referenced to fuller and somewhat different treatment in other 21s, which include longer workshops with smaller numbers.

We all have our own styles, and these bits of advice fit mine. They may not fit yours. Do your own thing in your own way.

Contents

1 Warn and prepare [see 2]

Warn. Make a list of what is required, and get it to the convenors and organizers well in advance.

Cost and access. Try to ensure that participation is free or nearly free. Charges tend to exclude students, the unwaged and younger people. Much of the point of these notes is to show that little is lost and much gained if more people come rather than fewer.

Space. A large flat room is best, with plenty of space but not so big that you need a microphone, and with plenty of walls for sticking up flip chart sheets, wall charts, photograph displays, etc. Best if it will blackout, if slides are to be shown. If there has to be a microphone, try for the clip-on mobile type that leaves you free to move around.

Drugs and calories. Ensure coffee, tea and lunch breaks. Have these where possible close by or in the room. Sandwiches save time at lunch. In countries and cultures with high caffeine addiction, insist that these be available on continuous tap or at suitable intervals. (Withdrawal symptoms can manifest in Scandinavia as early as 10:30am.) Smokers also need time out. Be alert for the signs of deprivation (fidgeting, twitching, rolling eyes, gasping …). If you go to 11:15 or 15:45 without space for fixes, expect trouble.

Start. Ask for no opening ceremony or speeches.

Names and contacts. Arrange early on that someone makes a list of names and contacts of participants and that this will be available to all by the time they are leaving.

2 Relate numbers and space

Large numbers can generate a lively atmosphere. Space and sound matter. Complaints about too many people are usually less linked to total numbers than to crowdedness (more often) or poor acoustics (less common). An ideal is to have as much free space behind the chairs as they themselves occupy. But this is not essential. You can run a workshop with a room full of chairs. It simply needs good space and sequence management (see below). It is a shame for people who want to come to a workshop to be kept out for real or supposed lack of room.

SPACE

Sometimes organizations or course organizers want to limit participation to 'their' people. This is against the spirit of sharing. Resist. Sometimes people on courses are saturated with some of their colleagues and only too delighted to meet and mix with others.

Tips

- When in doubt, invite and welcome more people. Numbers and diversity energize and stimulate.
- Find space (eg underneath tables by the walls) for personal impedimenta [see **10**].

3 Arrange the room [see **12**]

Do this the night before, or get in really early in the morning. Ask for helpers. There are many seating arrangements. An arrangement I now like is tables around the walls and chairs in several U-shaped rows facing a screen or board. If possible leave space behind the chairs for group activities.

Tips

- Leave big notices asking for the seating to be left as you have arranged it. Even so don't be surprised when you come back to find the classroom/opening ceremony default mode restored. Gnashing of teeth and tearing of hair ...
- Don't leave anything valuable overnight in a room, especially if it (what is left) is a bit tatty.[1]

4 Be optimally unprepared

Resist the temptation to plan everything in advance. Be ready with a repertoire but not a rigid programme. Improvise. Adapt. Treat the workshop as process not blueprint. Have things like slides, overheads and wall charts prepared. Alternate plenary and group activities in sequences (see 13 below) to give you time to regroup, change and prepare. Put up a chart showing only an outline programme so that you have flexibility within it.

5 Welcome and warm up [see **5**]

Put up a welcome notice. Organize early comers to welcome others and, as they arrive, give them:

---

1 In a hotel in Quebec I left my wall charts with a large sign in my best French: LAISSEZ SVP. The next morning I had to strip to underpants and dig with my hands for half an hour to retrieve them from the underground garbage tunnel. Two baths got rid of the smell but not the cuts from broken glass.

1   adhesive labels, and ask them to write their names on with big pens and stick on their clothing (the standard sticky labels which come in rolls stay stuck surprisingly long). Put one on yourself.

2   Post-its or their equivalent, and ask participants to write either their expectations from the workshop, or their hopes (on one Post-it) and fears (on another) and stick these up.

For starting, a short checklist is:

ADHESIVE LABELS

* welcome
* introductions [see **5**:6; **5**:8; **5**:9; **5**:10; and **5**:11]
* practise clapping (see 7 below)
* administration and logistics
* background to the workshop
* review of expectations, hopes and fears
* outline of the programme
* contract for when to end
* information – on documents, sources, videos.

Tips

* Avoid registration at the beginning, still more the collection of any payment for lunch. These can jam up a bottleneck and delay starting.
* Ensure enough entrance space to prevent a queue.
* Go for a relaxed and friendly start. What happens in the first half hour sets the tone for the whole workshop.
* Start participatory introductions while late arrivals are still coming in. Choose early activities (as above) which those who are late can join without difficulty or embarrassment, and missing some of which will not much matter. Make those who come late welcome.

6 Make a contract [see **5**:18]

When discussing the outline programme, ask when most people want to finish and seek consensus. Commit to finishing at that time. I am terrible at ending on time, which is why I need a contract. If you are well disciplined, you may not require this rigmarole.

Tips

* If participants want to finish rather too early in your view, and you think they may change their minds, say that the decision can be reviewed, for example, before breaking for lunch.

- I have tried saying that I will stay on after the end with whoever wants more time, but this rarely works. There is usually too much tidying up, and most people are tired and need to relax with a drink or whatever, or to catch a bus/train/plane.

7 Practise clapping for crowd (and dominator) control

Noise varies with participation. A big group is difficult to silence suddenly. With many noisy activities, you need a way to get quiet quickly. A participatory way is to start a slow handclap in which all join, speeding up and stopping suddenly. Practise this at the start. When the rapid claps cease there *should* (!) be silence, though normally pins would still drop unheard.

Tell participants they can use this to shut up you or any other big talker, or to end an activity. Be prepared for them to do so, and take it as a compliment!

8 Use wall posters

I use wall posters (flip chart sheets with large writing, or with photograph prints stuck on them) more than slides or overhead transparencies (though still using a few of those) because wall posters that do not fall down:

- stay there and can be looked at or copied from at leisure, whereas slides and transparencies flip on and off;
- decentre the room, moving attention round to where they are;
- can present outputs of group activities (eg participatory lists of dos and don'ts);
- allow or require wake-up movement and standing in going to look at them or explaining them.

Tips

- Build up a collection of posters. If you use overhead projector transparencies, progressively redraw them on flip charts.
- Keep them in a roll, and have a suitcase in which they fit.
- Use masking tape for putting them up. On most walls it leaves no mark. Place strips diagonally up and out from the top corners of charts. As rates of unpeeling are environment-specific, identify quickly whether you need more tape on the wall or on the chart. Go round and press down the tops and bottoms of the masking tape when it starts to uncurl.
- When taking posters down, either fold the tape back to make a tab for future use, or remove it altogether. Otherwise posters stick together and tear. Stop others taking them down unless they know this.
- If wall space is inadequate, try sticking charts on upended tables on top of other tables. This also reduces the space taken by the tables.
- Always have more rolls of masking tape than you expect to need.
- Have a place on your person (I have a dungaree-type pocket) where you always keep a spare roll of masking tape. You won't always keep it, but it helps to try. They have an astonishing tendency to disappear.

- Keep your cool when posters fall down. Make zero tolerance the order of the day. Stick them up again at once and never give up unless it is completely hopeless, in which case take them all down and find somewhere to spread them on the floor.

9 Foster participation in the workshop

Do not do yourself what others can do. Ask people to move furniture, prepare slips of paper, put up and take down displays, write up lists on flip charts as others call out, receive feedback, and so on.

Identify and involve those with experience. Ask, for example. 'Who here has experience of participatory approaches, methods and behaviours?' Then welcome the experience as a resource for the whole group.

Tips and options concerning those with experience

- In buzzes see that they are well distributed, where appropriate with one or more experienced person to each group.
- Ask them in plenary for their experience. If they are many, use hand raising. An example is 'Who has facilitated participatory mapping?' followed by 'Who has known people say they cannot make a map?' (usually most of them) followed by, 'And in the event could they make a map?' (usually all 'yes'). One or two can then describe the experience.
- Where several participants have good in-depth experience to share, let each have a place and groups rotate round them. Allow enough time for this.

Tip with video

- Show a video in the second half of a lunch break. Say that it is fine for people to return in the middle. At the end of the video ask those who saw all or most of it to share in small groups with those who came in later.

10 Maximize space [see 12]

Don't be stressed by lack of space. Managing it is fun. When a room looks too cramped, you can:

- Find another room.[2]
- Get rid of tables and big chairs. Or put tables round the edges of the room. Or upend them on top of one another and use them for wall charts.
- Ask that rucksacks, bags, coats, scarves, sandwiches, thermos flasks, soft drinks, books, umbrellas, cycle helmets, pets and other impedimenta be kept outside the room, or under tables round the edges.

---

2 This may be essential. In a Cairo hotel I was taken to the sixth floor to be shown the room for a workshop. My guide opened the door on a hotel bedroom with double bed. Tearing hair, I said 'But there may be 20 or 30 of us!' Ever helpful and unruffled he replied: 'I fetch extra bed?'

- Anticipate times when free floor space will be needed. Ask people to stack or remove chairs in advance.
- Pack as much as you can into dead space (corners, behind or in front of a screen, etc).
- Use walls outside the room for displays.[3]
- Use tables around the edges for sitting on.
- Go outside.

11 Manage movement [see 6 and 11]

Movement makes a workshop lively. Movement can be anything from turning around in a chair to look at something behind, to moving chairs to form small groups, getting up and walking around looking at things, or going outside. And all energizers involve some movement.

Tips

- Insist that chairs are moved for buzzes and groups.
- Make space. Shift or stack chairs if necessary.
- Use space to alternate activities. If there is empty space behind the chairs, move back and forth between sitting on the chairs and doing something in the space (brainstorming with flip charts on the ground, brief energizers etc).
- Use the ground.

GET UP AND LOOK

3 But beware. In the headquarters of an aid agency I stuck up grotty old charts in the passage. They disappeared. They had been removed on the orders of the Permanent Secretary who was expecting a visitor from the Prime Minister's office. This was, alas, unlikely to have advanced the career prospects of my sponsor.

- Show a slide with small detail and ask everyone to come close and look, getting them out of their chairs.
- Put up posters and ask people to get up and come and look (this can be planned in advance in placing the posters).

12 Galvanize graveyards [see **6** and **17**]

Anticipate troughs when blood sugar bottoms, energy sags, eyelids droop and attention strays. When a morning is to end at about 13:00, a common trough comes at around 12:15–12:45. The worst is the 'graveyard' of the early afternoon, between about 14:30 and 15:30. This can be tough. A hospitable lunch or alcohol aggravates the problem.

Tackle these bad times head on. The antidotes are activities and adrenalin.

Tips

- Limit lecturing. The victims can bear less than usual.
- Keep subjects with wall posters for the sleepy times. Put these up at the back and sides of the room so that all have to get up, move and stand to see them.
- Introduce SOSOTEC (see 17 below) activities (but judge this with care – one form of individual self-organization is sleep).
- Use energizers, jokes and teasers.
- Practise paradoxical prophylaxis: give permission to sleep, but urge to wake a neighbour gently if he (more rarely she) starts snoring.
- Ask someone else to take the session. Flatter. Say that only someone with her/his experience and skill can handle such a challenging time. This will allow you to sneak off and snooze yourself.

13 Structure sequences

Enjoy playing with sequences of subjects and activities. These are not modules, but flows which follow on from one another, each preparing for the next. Some examples:

- Space out breaks and buzzes, both for variety and to give yourself time to regroup and prepare for what is to come.
- Make sequences of space, activity and adrenalin. For example, before group brainstorming on the ground, circle chairs (clears central space) for 'jungle/fruit salad/vegetable soup' [see **11**:4] (wakes everyone up) leading to random groups for the activity on the ground in the space.
- A walk-around looking at photographs or wall charts which leads to brainstorming in groups and then plenary sharing.
- After an experiential exercise (like 'Saboteur' or 'Dominator' [see **18**:2 and **18**:3], or mapping a home neighbourhood) invite individual reflection, then sharing in small groups and sometimes plenary.

- Arrange variable activities (eg practicals) so that they run into breaks: this saves time, and also gives an incentive to groups to finish (the coffee/tea is getting cold/running out).
- Use the latter part of any break for an optional activity, open to those who are keen. A video for the second half of a lunch break is an example.

14 Talk and then buzz [see **17**:5–10]

A crucial sequence, deserving a separate heading. Say at the outset that you will never talk for more than 'n' minutes (brilliant if n<15) and that your talking will be followed by a buzz.

Tips for buzz groups

- Be sure to warn that they are coming. This encourages active listening.
- Insist that chairs are moved to make equilateral triangle trios.
- Demonstrate first the 'Wimbledon watching tennis' syndrome when seated in a line (the person in the middle gets plenty of neck exercise).
- Remember Eliot's law, that except for pairs, the number in a buzz group tends to exceed the number specified. Opinions differ on a good number. I like threes for buzzes – they give a quick start and full participation. But remember – if you ask for threes, expect some fours, and even fives.

TALK AND BUZZ

- Form topic buzz groups centred on participants with experience or knowledge.
- Don't feel you always have to follow a buzz with a plenary discussion [see **18**].

15 Jokes and teasers

Jokes are jokes. Teasers are puzzles for participants to guess. In PRA/PLA-related workshops, 'Whose Reality?' teasers fit well. Collect examples from field experience, Participatory Poverty Assessments and the like, where people have presented a surprising reality. This can be, for instance, an unanticipated criterion in matrix scoring, an unexpected reason for doing something, or an unforeseen perceived priority [see **14**]. If you are bold and either foolhardy or rich, put some money on it and bet participants that they will not be able to guess.

Tips

- Neighbours can form syndicates to guess.
- Congratulate anyone who guesses right.

- Invite reflection afterwards on how little we know.
- With currencies other than your own, get the decimal point in the right place.[4]

16 Rapid listing

Ask participants to make rapid lists. Either start with individual lists which are then shared in groups, or start straight away in groups.

There is a surprising number of topics on which people can generate their own lists instead of having to be shown or taught. They include:

- criteria for making a judgement;
- dos and don'ts for almost any social activity;
- advantages and disadvantages of alternatives;
- how to deal with a difficult situation;
- and so on. (Make your own rapid list!)

To share lists quickly, volunteers writing on flip charts, eliciting from groups in turn, is probably the best combination of speed, effectiveness and participation [see **15**:14].

17 SOSOTEC (Self-Organizing Systems On The Edge of Chaos)

[See **12**:15 and **14**:16–20.] In SOSOTEC, each person decides for herself what to do. SOSOTEC may be simply time and space to walk around and look at materials and wall charts. SOSOTEC can be for PRA/PLA method practicals. In the past I used to organize these with detailed briefing. Now I have found that they can be self-organizing. For matrix scoring, I used to take 20 minutes to explain. Now all that seems to be needed is a few wall charts and photographs, a few examples of items to compare and an invitation to form groups. Anyone with an idea of a set of items to compare convenes a group of others who are interested. It works. Amazing. Much more is probably waiting for self-organization. Explore. And watch this space.

Clearing up and restoring what remains of the furniture to its previous pattern can be done by self-organizing volunteers.

18 Queue to speak

This is a neat, low stress way of enhancing the quality of shared reflection and feedback with large numbers. Once started it runs itself. Place a table centrally with three or four chairs. Arrange the other chairs in one or more big circles around the table. Have microphones if there is a crowd. Whoever wishes can sit down and speak. Those in the chairs take turns. Others who wish to speak stand and queue behind them. If anyone speaks too long, the person standing behind gives a gentle tap on the shoulder (laughter often follows, and a quick good-humoured termination by the talker).

Source: World Bank Participation Workshop, 1995

4 In Finland I got the decimal point in the wrong place, lost a teaser and embarrassed my hosts socially and myself financially because of the large sum I had to insist the winner take.

19 Questions and issues: ration and respond [see 7:15]

Questions, queries and criticisms often need to be raised, but with large numbers in plenary they can deflect, delay and distract. You can postpone them to a final session, but this is often squeezed for time. This can trap you into lecturing. Four ways of rationing questions and issues and restraining your responses are:

PARKING PLACE

1   *Plenary free-for-all.* This is really a plenary free-for-a-few. The same few people tend to ask questions or raise issues while most remain silent and even look resentful. Also, you have no warning of what is coming up. All the same, this is the simplest method.
2   *Parking place.* Postpone questions and issues as they arise, asking questioners to write them on cards. Collect and cluster these. Invite all to mark their most important cards. Respond to those cards only [see 7:15].
3   *Group and ration.* Form groups and let each decide on and raise one question or issue.
4   *Groups select and share.* Let groups form around single questions or issues of their choice. Invite the groups to debate among themselves first and then share with the plenary.

Tips and options

*   Preserve time for this part, working backwards from when the workshop or session must close.
*   Keep your responses brief.
*   Identify questions and issues that lead into what you want to say at the end, and when they come up, defer them.

20 Reflection and evaluation [see 7 and 16:19]

Among many options some of the most suitable for large numbers are the following:

*   Silent individual reflection followed by quiet discussion in small groups.
*   One or more large sheets listing the sessions stuck up near the door(s) to be scored as people leave.
*   Scribbled notes left on a chair by the door [see 7:3].

Remember that in a large group one or two people may make sharp comments which represent only a small minority view, and that those who were really fed up have usually left or will not take part.

21 Ignore all the above and invent, experiment, for yourself

Every time try something new. Do your own thing. And fail forwards.

Part 5
Analysis and Learning

14

21 of the Best

This is a collection of favourites for experiencing, analysing and learning. They vary in aims, length and the types of experience, analysis and learning to which they give access.

May this encourage you to collect and create your own 21 of the Best, adding to and improving on what is here, and sharing what you do.

Contents

These 21 fall into four sets.

Multiple realities

Expression and awareness of different realities.

1   Whose reality? teasers
2   Whose way up?
3   Johari's window
4   If I were you...
5   Images
6   Arguing the opposite

Experiential communication and learning

Exercises for active learning by doing.

7   One minute flat
8   PRA visuals practicals
9   PRA mini-process
10 Being taught to do it yourself

Cooperation and groups

Games that explore the costs of conflict and the potential of cooperation.

11 Kim's game
12 Knotty problem
13 My corner
14 Cooperative squares
15 Contested chairs

SOSOTEC

Self-organizing systems on the edge of chaos, in which each person decides for herself what to do within a framework of minimal rules and timetabling.

16 Card writing, sorting and consensus
17 Open space
18 Share fair
19 Self-organizing collection and synthesis
20 Clearing up
21 Make your own collection

MULTIPLE REALITIES

1 Whose reality? Teasers

Fun ways for appreciating how hard it is to know the realities of others unless they show and tell us. Examples of teasing questions or teasers are given below. Present the teaser and invite perhaps ten or 20 guesses. Then draw out the lessons, that local people know their realities and priorities, and we do not. Our guesses are often wrong.

Examples

- In a village in an irrigated area in Gujarat, a line of tamarind trees between a dirt road and the fields was being cut down. Why?
- In Sulawezi, Indonesia, separate groups of livestock extension staff and villagers did matrix scoring to compare characteristics of different types of domestic animals – ducks, hens, buffalo, goats, horses and cattle. One characteristic was very important to villagers, but not thought of by any of five groups of livestock extension staff. Can you guess what it was?
- A mother in Norway did matrix scoring for the different foods she gave her children aged one and three. She had one criterion I would never have thought of but which other mothers might share. What do you think it was?
- Maasai herdsmen in Tanzania did matrix scoring for different sources of fodder for their cattle. They compared for one characteristic that few non-pastoralists would ever think of. Can you imagine what it was?
- In a Participatory Poverty Assessment in Bangladesh, very poor urban women listed and ranked 'do-ables' – changes they felt were feasible and would make their lives better. Their first was water. Can you guess their second and third?
- What did villagers in Bolivia give as their priority when asked how their environment could be improved?
- In a village in Karnataka, goats had half a coconut shell tied round their necks. Why?
- When street lighting was installed in Anantapur, a city in India, women in one area were pleased but in another threw stones and broke the lights. Why?
- Can you complete this sentence in a report from Ndola, Zambia: 'The poorest depend on ....'?

(For the answers, see the end of this 21.)

Tips

- Invite participants to brainstorm and guess in pairs.
- Risk a small sum, betting that participants will not guess.
- Invite participants to pose their own teasers (this may also add to your stock).
- Build up your own collection of teasers. Some likely sources are:
  - ask people questions about their lives, livelihoods and experiences; some replies are usually unexpected;
  - matrix scoring, for unexpected criteria or weightings;

- transect walks, for unexpected objects, uses, explanations;
- problem (and solution) listing and ranking, for unexpected problems (and solutions);
- slides can sometimes provide 'what is it?' or 'what is happening?' or 'what do you see?' teasers.

2 Whose way up?

A simple, short, striking and memorable way to illustrate how differently we see things, depending on who and where we are. (A year later this was almost the only thing a group of students could remember from a whole workshop.)

All you need is a large map (eg of the world or of the country) with which participants are familiar. Hold the map up 'upside down' for the participants. Propeller-like hand movements will usually tell you to turn it 'the right way up'. 'What's the problem?' It's upside down'. Look down at it in innocence. 'No it isn't'.

Discussion can be linked to uses of the word 'remote' or its equivalents in other languages. 'We' use remote to mean far from where we are, which is almost always in an urban centre. To distant villagers it is the urban centre that is remote.

Variant or addition:

Hand out a blank outline map of the country. Ask people to put it with South at the top and North at the bottom and then write in the main cities and/or area names. Astonishingly some may not do this but will turn the map the 'normal' way round. Discuss how deeply habitual our ways of seeing things are, and how difficult it is to see things differently.

Source: Kamal Kar in *Participatory Learning and Action: A Trainer's Guide* [see **21**:1, p205].

3 Johari's window

A versatile framework to enhance awareness of the differences between professionals' and local people's knowledge. Show a two-by-two matrix.

	They know	They don't know
We know		
We don't know		

Ask participants to draw their own matrix and fill in items in the boxes, either generally for professionals and local people, or for specific sorts of professionals (administrators, agricultural scientists, service providers) and others (poor people, resource-poor farmers, users of services).

Share these. The usual outcome is that the box where they know and we do not is larger than expected.

Tips

- Invite reflection on which boxes flatter our egos, which boxes we assume to be largest, and what behaviours go with the different boxes.

Sources: Many, including *Participatory Learning and Action: A Trainer's Guide* [see **21**:1, p203], and traceable back to J Luft (1970) *Group Processes: An Introduction to Group Dynamics.*

4 If I were You.....

An exercise for imagining, learning and appreciating the realities of others.

1 The group chooses a statement to work with, beginning with 'If I were you …'. Two common choices are: 'If I were you, a main concern of mine would be …' or 'If I were you one of my main goals would be …'
2 Each member writes her/his name on two slips of paper. These are put in a hat, pot or other suitable container.
3 Each draws out two slips, returning or trading with someone else if it is her/his own name.
4 Each in turn is the person in focus. The two who have the focus person's name slips complete 'If I were you…'
5 After listening to both, the focus person responds.
6 Finally all reflect on the activity and any new insights they have gained.

Source: adapted slightly from *Facilitator's Guide to Participatory Decision Making* [see **21**:8, p174].

5 Images

An absorbing, even riveting, source of awareness of how different groups see one another. Divide into groups according to type, often type of organization (eg government, INGOs, NGOs, donors). It is easiest with only two types, but three is possible. The description that follows is for two groups.

Each group takes a flip chart sheet (or two or more taped together), draws three columns and brainstorms adjectives that describe:

1 how they see themselves (column one), and then
2 how they see the other group (column two), and then
3 how they think the other group sees them (column three).

Display and compare the sheets. Invite reflection and comment. Considerable discussion can ensue. Allow plenty of time for this, with groups separate or all together depending on dynamics and purpose.

Tips and options

- Loosen up with an energizer before this. It is better in, say, the second half of a one-day workshop, when participants have met on a friendly basis and relaxed a bit.
- Allow anything from 30 to 90 minutes, or even more for follow-up discussions.
- With three types or groups, several combinations are possible. If the groups are A, B and C, the most symmetrical arrangement is for each group to split into two. This makes six groups – A1, A2, B1, B2, C1 and C2. A1's analysis can then relate to group B and A2's to group C; B1's to A and B2's to C; and C1's to A and C2's to B.
- Keep a record and later send a consolidated copy, showing the comparisons, to all participants.

6 Arguing the opposite

When fully acted out, a powerful way to discover and empathize with a point of view opposed to one's own. Explain the exercise carefully.

Each participant chooses a personal disagreement with a belief, action or point of view generally, or with a person with whom they have a problem but who is not present. Place two chairs facing each other. One chair (A) is for the participant's point of view. The other chair (B) is for the view or person disagreed with. In turn, participants sit in A and put their case to the empty chair B, which represents the other view or person. They then sit in B and reply with the other view, or the view of the other person, showing how they see and feel things.

Tips and options

- Allow 30 to 90 minutes.
- Make a judgement about how public this can or should be. It can be done with pairs, with one talking and one observing, or with threes with each in turn talking while the other two observe.
- The experience can be quite deep. Allow time for quiet reflection. It is a pity to rush this.
- Threes will vary in the time they take. Have a follow-on activity for those that finish first.
- Some people may find this difficult. Understand their problem and encourage them to observe others and to reflect.
- A variant is for someone else to sit in the A chair and argue back as though they were the participant, who still argues the opposite of what she/he believes or the view of the person with whom there is a disagreement or problem.

EXPERIENTIAL COMMUNICATION AND LEARNING

7 One minute flat

Explores the potential for quick, effective and memorable communication. Small teams form and decide a message which they will illustrate and present in one minute flat. The presentation can take any form – acting, showing, speaking. Teams prepare and then present. After each presentation ask what the message was.

Finally discuss which were the more memorable and why. What is there to learn about how we communicate? Do we often talk too much? Do soundbites oversimplify?

Examples

- Whose way up? (see 1 above)
- Mumble about communication inaudibly, looking downwards, fidgeting etc. After 50 seconds (it seems a long time!), look up and say: 'To communicate, look up, look the other person in the eye, and say something short and clear' (or words to that effect).
- 'Your standpoint is your viewpoint'. A and B sit or stand facing each other, A with back to door, B facing the door. C asks 'where is the door?' A says 'behind'. B says 'in front'. C repeats the question. A and B end up shouting at each other.

Tip

- Encourage some, if not all, of the groups to use theatre.
- If theatre is used, allow perhaps half an hour for preparation.

Source: Training for Transformation [see **21**:9, Vol 1, p75]; and Alan Margolis.

8 PRA visuals practicals

To give participants an opportunity to practice and experience one or more PRA visual methods for analysis and presentation. Materials can be the ground and natural things like sticks, stones, leaves and/or:

- flip charts;
- marker pens (coloured as well as black);
- chalks (coloured as well as white);
- seeds (of several sorts, large and flattish being best);
- scissors, glue and coloured papers that can be cut into shapes are also sometimes useful.

There are many ways to do this. Keep on developing your own. Some options are:

Choice of process

- All do the same method. Proceed in sequence through different methods; or

- Do different methods simultaneously. In this case either: post signs for different methods in different places; participants choose with their feet; or groups self-form to do methods they choose.

Briefing

- I used to give detailed briefing. Now I have found that groups can be largely self-organizing (see 16–19 below). For matrix scoring, I used to take 20 minutes to explain. Now all that seems needed is a few wall charts and photographs, a few examples of items to compare and an invitation to form groups. Anyone with an idea of a set of items to compare convenes a group of others who are also interested.

Methods (short list only)

- Mapping – social, resource, mobility, health, etc.
- 3-D modelling of an environment.
- Timeline.
- Matrix scoring.
- Card sorting and ranking.
- Personal time use analysis.
- Venn (chapati/tortilla/dumpling) (institutional) diagramming.
- Causal and linkage diagramming.
- Trend and change diagramming.
- Seasonal calendar diagramming.
- For a practical guide to visual methods see *Embracing Participation in Development: Wisdom from the Field* [see **21**:4, Part 3].

Place

- The ground or floor is often best (see 16 below).
- Go out of doors or have out of doors as an option.
- Use passages, flat roofs, etc.

Time

- Usually one method can be practised in 15–20 minutes if a group gets its act together.

Tips and options

- These activities can be for anything from 20 minutes to a day depending on how many methods are used.
- Ask who has experience and invite them to help.
- For good participation, keep group size down to three or four, at most five.
- Do not give too much briefing. Let participants experiment, invent, make mistakes and discover for themselves.
- Those who finish early can move on to another method.

- Either have a SOSOTEC (see below) move around to see what others have done (takes less time, but less learning), or all visit each method and have a presentation and discussion (often good, but can take a long time).
- Run this activity into a tea/coffee break so that groups can finish at different times and all start together afterwards.
- At the end show and explain that there are many ways in which methods can be applied, and many forms they can take.
- Reject the above and make your own list of tips. There is no one right way to do this.

9 PRA mini-process

Experience of using visuals in an analytical sequence leading to reflection about realities and processes. Here is an example.

Have paper and pen for each participant, small or cut up Post-its, and two types of seeds.

1 Mapping (10–15 minutes)

- Ask participants to draw a sketch map of the neighbourhood, environment and facilities around where they live. This can be home for anyone living temporarily away from home. Stress environment and facilities. Give a time limit of, say, three minutes. Encourage use of the whole of the paper. Warn as the time is coming to an end.
- They share with neighbours.
- Ask what types of details they have shown and who has shown them.
- Ask how many have maps oriented with north at the top and south at the bottom. (The worldwide average seems to be about 20 per cent, so that about 80 per cent have another orientation.) Then elicit discussion of how local people, with similar mental maps, may find 'our' official maps difficult because they are differently oriented. Note that this is a general point about how we present and try to share knowledge expressed in 'our' way.

2 Analysis, scoring and action (15–20 minutes)

Ask participants to:

- Think of three improvements they would like in their environment, and locate these on their maps with Post-it strips.
- Take a set number of seeds (say at least seven) and allocate them to the improvements to show their relative importance (eg four on one, two on another and one on the third, or any combination of scoring).
- Show to neighbours and explain and discuss.
- Repeat with different coloured seeds for relative feasibility of the improvement.
- Again show to neighbours, explain and discuss.

Then elicit discussion of the process, including the advantages of visuals and scores that are easy to change.

3 Reflection and sharing (10–15 minutes)

At the end, set aside two to three minutes for silent individual reflection on the experience – what happened, what have you learnt, what was it like, do you see anything differently? – followed by quiet sharing with neighbours and perhaps also in plenary.

Options and tips

• Can be done on the ground instead of paper.
• With paper, half a flip chart sheet is a good size, allowing enough space for the Post-its and seeds.
• With paper, encourage drawing sitting on the floor (easier to share).

10 Being taught to do it yourself

A powerful and enjoyable reversal of roles in a community, often as part of PRA training, learning about the skills of others, one's own clumsiness, and the fun of being taught something new [see **18**:8].

Allow anything up to six hours or even a full day. In a field situation with a community, say one hour preparation, three hours practicals and interactions with community members and one–two hours video playback and discussion. This can also be done on the spur of the moment as opportunity arises. When it is organized:

• Identify tasks and willing teachers. In an agricultural village, tasks may be, for example, transplanting rice, thatching a hut, washing clothes, fishing, ploughing, using a winnowing tray (looks easy, fiendishly difficult to do well), cooking a meal.
• List the tasks and invite participants to sign up for one or more.
• The tasks are taught and performed.
• Discuss the experience.
• Invite the local teachers to give feedback to participants.

Video option

• Ask people in the community if it is all right to take a video. (In practice, I have found that videos are perceived as less intrusive than cameras.)
• Brief a video camera person(s) to know what to look for and capture.
• Preview the video. It may be necessary to fast-forward over sections that might too seriously embarrass anyone.
• Playback the video and discuss the experience.
• Show the video to community members. This can lead to much hilarity and can be a way of giving something back and saying thank you.

- Invite community members to comment to the participants on what they observed.

Tips

- Explain that this is a reversal of roles, important in participatory orientation and training, and widely practised around the world.
- Avoid oversubscription to the easier and cleaner tasks!
- Set a personal example. Help and encourage any participants who have difficulties.
- Ethics. Be sensitive about taking the time of community members, and about their property. Anticipate, prevent, minimize and/or compensate for damage. In Bihar a field of paddy clumsily 'transplanted' by trainee outsiders was retransplanted by the farmer (for whom, however, providing free entertainment to the village may have made up for the labour).

KIM'S GAME

COOPERATION AND GROUPS

11 Kim's game

A game that illustrates how a group knows more than an individual, and how members of a group can help each other to remember. Collect about 30–40 different objects which can be displayed together. Divide into actors and observers. Display the objects for a short time (say two–three minutes) where everyone can see them. Then remove them from view.

Ask the actors to list what they can remember, some as individuals and some in one or more groups. Ensure that the other group(s) and individuals are all out of earshot.

Compare the results. Usually the groups are much more successful than the individuals. Discuss how:

1   several people know more than one person;
2   interactive processes can bring out more than just the sum of what individuals know or can do.

Tips

- Have a few observers who note and report back on group processes.
- Allow 20–30 minutes.

Source: Traditional. See also Action Speaks Louder: A Handbook of Structured Group Techniques [see **21**:15, pp72–3].

12 Knotty problem

An old favourite that shows how people can (often, usually) solve their problems faster and better on their own than when instructed by outsiders. Powerful when combined with reflective discussion and a good energizer.

Select one or a few participants to be managers. The remaining participants hold hands (and must not let go) and still holding hands work themselves into as complicated a tangle as they can. Ask

KNOTTY PROBLEM

the managers, hands behind their backs and without touching, to unravel the knot using verbal instructions only. Tell the participants to do only what they are told. Time the untangling. It usually takes three or more minutes, if it occurs at all.

Repeat the tangling. This time tell the group to untangle themselves. Usually it takes 20–30 seconds only. Invite discussion of the significance of the experience (eg what does this tell us about participation? About the roles of 'outsiders' and 'insiders'? About facilitating local development?).

Tips and options

- Allow 10–15 minutes.
- Check that none of the managers knows the exercise.
- Be sensitive to gender and culture. In some contexts those tangling should be all men or all women. Those who do not take part can be managers or observers.
- Invite the managers to join in and to be part of the second knot.

Source: Adapted from *Participatory Learning and Action: A Trainer's Guide* [see **21**:1].

13 My corner

A quick activity that highlights how collaboration can reconcile conflicting individual goals. Ask the group to form a circle holding hands. Each person chooses a corner of the room that is 'theirs'. Each must then visit their corner without breaking the circle. Individuals often doggedly try to persuade everyone to go to their corner and their corner only, rather than visit each in turn. Discuss.

Source: Participatory Learning and Action: A Trainer's Guide, citing Alan Margolis [see **21**:1, p177].

14 Cooperative squares

An activity rich in lessons about cooperation, communication and ourselves. Allow one hour or more (five–ten minutes briefing, 20 minutes exercise, 15–20 minutes for group discussions, and 15–20 for plenary and reflection).

In advance, cut five squares into pieces as in the diagram. Cut them exactly. All cuts are to corners or the middle of sides. Mix the pieces up and put them in five

COOPERATIVE SQUARES

envelopes. (Option: in one of the envelopes put only one piece.) Repeat until there are enough sets for all participants in teams of five with an observer for each team.

Process:

1   Form groups of six, each with five participants and one observer.
2   Brief all as follows:
   - Each group member will have one envelope containing pieces. The task is to form five squares of *equal size* from the pieces, one for each group member.
   - No one may speak or communicate in any way, or help others to make their squares.
   - No one may take a piece but pieces can be given away.
   - The task is finished when each group member has completed a square.
   - There are 10–20 minutes to complete the task.
3   Brief the observers separately. Their task is to watch, note and then facilitate group discussion at the end, feeding back their observations, tactfully where necessary. They should focus on positive aspects before negative, and encourage people to discuss their own behaviour. Laughter helps (the exercise is fun as well as serious).
4   Give the observers a note like the following (This is simply an example. One you make up yourself may be better): 'Make notes on the points below, and anything else significant about the group's behaviour. Watch hands and eyes, what people are feeling and how they express their feelings. Look out for:
   - How do degrees of willingness to share differ, and how are these expressed?
   - When does the group start to cooperate, and what makes this happen?
   - Does the person with only one piece behave differently?
   - Does anyone hide their pieces from the others?
   - Does anyone keep lots of pieces all the time?
   - Does anyone give away all their pieces? What happens then?

- Does anyone complete a square and sit back uninterested in the others?
- Does anyone keep their completed square when others see they are preventing completion of the task? How do people behave when this happens?
- If someone's square has to be broken so that all can finish, how do they react?'

5   Start the exercise. Allow it to go on as long as needed.
6   Observers debrief and facilitate their groups.
7   Share and discuss in plenary.

Tips and options

- Be cautious about exposing individuals. Individual behaviour is usually better discussed in group debriefing than in plenary unless those concerned raise it (which they may well do).
- Reports back can be on flip chart sheets or verbal.
- The plenary discussion can provide good opportunities for reflection and learning. Do not rush it. Issues that come up may include:
  - how we behave in groups;
  - non-verbal communication;
  - power and possessiveness: how unselfishness and personal disempowerment can lead to gains for all;
  - our deep feelings about participation;
- At the end, take two–three minutes for silent personal reflection with each person noting what they have experienced and learnt.

Sources: adapted from *Participatory Learning and Action: A Trainer's Guide* [see **21**:1, pp171–2] citing *Training for Transformation* [see **21**:9] (originally from J W Pfeiffer and J E Jones *Structured Experiences for Human Relations Training*, Vol 1); and personal communication, Mary Underwood.

15 Contested chairs

A game about conflict and cooperation.

Process

Allow 30–45 minutes.
1   Set out a number of chairs.
2   Prepare three sets of slips with instructions about what to do with the chairs.
3   Form three roughly equal groups.
4   Give each group slips with the same instructions, one copy for each person. Each group then has a different instruction about how to arrange the chairs, for example:
- Put all the chairs in a circle. *You have 15 minutes to do this.*
- Put all the chairs near the door. *You have 15 minutes to do this.*
- Put all the chairs near the window. *You have 15 minutes to do this.*
5   Tell them not to share the instructions with other groups.

6   Start.
7   Stop, reflect, discuss and analyse.

Comments

This exercise has great scope for creative conflict resolution. Groups often burst into frantic action, use force and sometimes carry chairs with others desperately sitting on them to their corner. When some participants are trying to find a cooperative solution, others can be seen continuing to collect and defend their chairs. This, in turn, frustrates the cooperators, who forget their positive intentions and join the argument [see **21**:1, p167].

The analysis can focus on aspects of the authority and interpretation of instructions; and on non-aggressive conflict resolution. The instructions cannot be carried out without cooperation within each group. The groups cannot all carry out their instructions without cooperation between groups. A surprisingly large number of solutions are possible, such as:

1   all chairs in a circle, between the door and window;
2   putting the chairs consecutively in a circle, then near the door, then near the window;
3   disobeying the instructions, and putting a third of the chairs in a circle, a third by the door and a third by the window;
4   renaming places by hanging flip charts in the middle of the room, one saying DOOR and the other WINDOW;
5   disobeying the instructions entirely and sitting down together.

Discussion and analysis

A checklist:

- What did you experience?
- How did you relate to those who wanted to do something else?
- If you confronted others, how did you do it?
- Did you follow instructions? Did you feel they had to be carried out whatever happened? Why (obedience, etc)?
- Was your behaviour influenced by your cultural background? Position in an organization?
- How would you do this another time?
- Can you relate this to real life situations?

Tips and options

- Appoint a few observer/analysts. Brief them on what to look for. Include as observers anyone who is disabled or liable to be distressed by moderate rough-and-tumble.
- Be gender sensitive. In some cultures men and women should not take part together.

- No talking. Then at a later stage allow talking within groups. Then talking between groups. Resolution of the conflicts through negotiation may then take place.
- Without talking between groups, encourage an exchange of diagrams.
- Have some Band-aid ready for minor abrasions.

Source: Quoting and adapted from *Participatory Learning and Action: A Trainer's Guide* [see **21**:1, pp167–8], citing Frank Oomkes and Richard Thomas (1992) *Cross-Cultural Communication: A Trainer's Manual*, Gower, Aldershot, UK.

SELF-ORGANIZING SYSTEMS ON THE EDGE OF CHAOS (SOSOTEC)

SOSOTEC is based on minimal rules and a skeleton timetable within which there is a high degree of autonomy for individuals to do what makes sense to them. It can be simply time and space to walk around and look at materials and wall charts. At its most complex it can lead to high degrees of spontaneously organized activity.

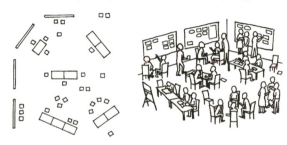

SOSOTEC

16 Card writing, sorting and consensus

A widely adaptable and versatile sequence of activities. Writing on cards and sorting them into lists, categories and relationships has become a common method in participatory training, workshops and practical analysis. It allows all participants (providing they can write) to share their ideas and wishes with others.

CARD WRITING AND SORTING

In the classic traditions of ZOPP and VIPP, a facilitator arranges the cards on a wall or board, asking for suggestions and comments from the group. Usually the facilitator stands while others sit. Cards and their positions are discussed one by one. This can be slow and tedious. The facilitator can easily slip into 'facipulating'. The more vocal and articulate participants tend to say most and have most influence. Facilitators are now increasingly using the ground, finding it quicker, more fun and more egalitarian. We can talk of the *democracy of the ground* [see **12**:18 and **19**:17].

Anyone can write a card and throw it down. The cards can be anonymous. Anyone can add a card when they see what is already there. Anyone can get down on the ground and start sorting the cards, identifying the categories in which they can be clustered. Anyone can move a card from one cluster to another. On the ground, those who are quieter tend to be relatively empowered and the bigger talkers relatively disempowered. Dominant people may remain standing and so be out of the action; and if they do get down and sort, it is harder to dominate on all fours and with less eye contact. Moving cards reduces talking. And much sorting goes on simultaneously. The outcome can be something close to a democratic consensus.

Process

Obtain cards or tear up flip charts or A4 paper (A5, that is, half A4, is a good size). Ensure plenty of marker pens and adequate ground space for sorting. Then:
1   Clarify the purpose and procedure. (Paired or small group discussions can help thinking before writing.)
2   Invite all individually or in small groups to write on the cards, with a separate card for each idea/question/wish, etc.
3   As they are written and become available, cards are thrown down on a large open area.
4   Any or all take part in sorting and grouping the cards on the ground. More cards can be added.
5   As cards are clustered, a title for each cluster is written boldly on a different sort of card. These cards go down as markers to help sort the rest.
6   Invite checking and changes.
7   Stick the results on a wall for all to see.
8   (*Option*) participants score the cards or clusters of cards for importance each using a fixed ration of stickers or marks with a pen.

Tips

*   Ensure that individuals know they can write their own cards even if they are working in groups.
*   All should use large markers and large or capital letters.
*   Only one point on one card. Ending up with a lot of cards is usually not a problem.
*   Try to have plenty of space all round for the sorting. More people can then see and also take part.
*   For clarity, save one colour of pen or paper for the headings. Be alert and ready, or have someone else alert and ready, to write out the headings as they emerge. This helps and speeds the sorting.
*   If many people (say over 50), or many cards (say over 120) are involved, a few participants can sort them while the rest continue with something else or during a tea/coffee or lunch break.
*   For wall display, cards can be stuck up in various ways including stringing on masking tape, or using adhesive spray.
*   Consider whether in displaying the clusters of cards there is a sequence (left to right on the wall) that makes sense.

- Beware of cards written early in a process being given too much importance later on when thinking has moved on. Deletions, rewriting and simply ignoring some are often needed as discussion and thinking evolve.

Applications

- Establishing the agenda for a participatory workshop [see **5**].
- Eliciting and consolidating points for an evaluation [see **7**].
- Sharing knowledge and ideas in processes of learning [see **16**].
- Consolidating and analysing complex data, and sharing knowledge and analysis of a subject [see **15**].
- Encouraging all to contribute ideas for action.
- Identifying critical issues, challenges or future priorities for an organization, as part of strategic planning.

One strong process is from *cards to consensus*.

This can help move towards democratic consensus about agendas, principles, precepts, and/or actions. Carefully handled, it allows shy people to raise issues anonymously. It is much faster and less contentious than debates conducted item by item.

The cards on the ground are sorted. Participants walk around, read, reflect and turn over or put a sticker or mark on any they disagree with or consider should be discussed. Those not turned over or marked are taken as agreed. Those turned over are then separated out, displayed and discussed one by one.

Tips

- Say at the outset that those who turn over or mark cards will be anonymous.
- Preserve this anonymity unless people voluntarily identify themselves; for example, 'I turned over that card. The reason is...'
- Ask whoever disagrees with a card to redraft it for reconsideration by the group. This can be done alone, or with volunteers, while the rest continue with the other cards (In a workshop in Nairobi this worked extremely well. Those redrafting sought compromise formulations in the hope of getting their amendments accepted.)

The method of turning over cards was used in May 1994 in the process which led to 'Sharing Our Concerns and Looking to the Future' (Absalom et al). See also 'Card Sorting on the Ground' (Chambers, 1997a).

17 Open space

A flexible, self-selecting process for identifying, exploring and sharing insights about issues and subjects people care about. Have ready as many flip charts and sets of markers as there are likely to be groups (often in the range of four–eight groups). Arrange space for the groups to meet without disturbing other groups. Allow anything from half an hour to a day.

Process

1   Explain the purpose and process, including what will happen at the end. The purpose is to enable groups to form around topics they care about.
2   Invite participants to identify and convene groups. Anyone can form a group around any subject. Would-be group convenors explain and display their topics and stand separately.
3   Participants join groups of their choice.
4   Groups do their thing, whatever it is, brainstorming, debating, discussing and then preparing to share.
5   Groups share (see also information market below). This can be:

   • all reporting in series; or
   • two or three reporting sessions of several groups in parallel, with a choice for participants of which groups to go to.

Attitudes that go with 'Open space' are:

• Whoever come are the right people.
• Whatever happens is the only way things could happen.
• Whenever it starts is the right time.
• When it is over, it is over.
• Follow the law of two feet. Choose your group, leave your group.

Source: Participation Works! [see **21**:5] which refers to Harrison Owen *Open Space Technology: A User's Guide*, and *Expanding Now: the Story of Open Space*. Price £17.99 plus p&p from Wikima, 23 Leamington Road Villas, London W11 1HS, tel/fax 0207 229 7320, email romys@compuserve.com.

18 Share fair

A way of sharing a range of information, materials, experience or insights with choices wide open to participants. Arrange a hall or open place suitable for setting up stalls, with rooms, videos, slide projectors, overhead projectors, tables, chairs, pinboards, pallets, as needed.
   Decide whether there will be set presentations at intervals, or whether it will be a wander around occasion. Arrange for the stalls to be set up

SHARE FAIR

Tips and options

• Inform participants in advance so that they come prepared with their displays.
• An obstinate weakness is that those presenting or at stalls are denied the opportunity to learn from others. Pairs or trios staffing stalls can take turns.
• Vaguely wandering around picking up leaflets which are then never read is inefficient. An initial guided tour followed by short and repeated set piece presentations at stalls can partly overcome this.

- Have a well displayed programme indicating what is happening when and where. Combine with a lecture, a play, a concert, a dance, a celebration, social events, refreshments and so on.
- Arrange places for ad hoc meetings with chairs in various loose groupings, tea and coffee, and maybe one or two tables.
- Create a relaxed and festive atmosphere with beach umbrellas, streamers and posters.

Sources: various, including the August 2000 Participatory Action Research Congress at the University of Ballarat, Australia.

19 Self-organizing collection and synthesis

A process for collecting and collating information, experience and contributions in a short time. This can be astonishingly effective under white-heat pressure when committed participants contribute freely and frankly to a harvest of experience and ideas for a synthesis or report.

Enabling conditions

- Committed and creative participants with initiative, stamina, enthusiasm and relevant experience and knowledge.
- Collection points. These can be wall charts, tables, areas of floor, people with laptops ...
- If laptops are being used, try to ensure reliable electricity or spare batteries, tables round a large room, access to plugs, converter plugs and extension leads as maybe, and one or more printers.
- A photocopier that does not break down can help.
- Anything from two to 48 hours.
- A good dose of luck that everything does indeed work.
- (For some) ample coffee, tea and other stimulants according to culture, ecology and taste.

Process

1 Discuss and agree purposes and topics (see 16 above). Besides card sorting this can include iterative discussion of:
   - feasibility of topics for collection and synthesis;
   - who the synthesis or report is for, and how it will be used;
   - the causal links between the report and the intended impact (a diagram showing causal linkages can help);
   - who is able and willing to champion topics;
   - length, style and format of contributions.
2 Identify volunteer topic champions and hunter-gatherer-collectors (two or three per topic can work well).
3 Champions provide organizing nodes. Others move around and contribute as they can in different ways in different places.

Tips

- Do not expect everyone to contribute equally. But if there has been an initial card writing and sorting it is likely that everyone can contribute something.
- Be inventive. From experience to date, every such occasion is likely to be highly idiosyncratic.
- Be open to change throughout.
- Reflect continuously on how what is collected is going to be processed further and used. Get as much as possible done on the spot before participants leave.

Two workshops that successfully used SOSOTEC for collection and synthesis have been the 1996 Bangalore and Madurai South–South Workshop on ABC of PRA [see **21**:7], and the June 1999 near-Delhi International Synthesis Workshop for the 23-country Consultations with the Poor.

20 Clearing up

At the end of a session, of a day, or of a longer workshop, there is often a lot of clearing up to be done – rubbish to be binned, charts to be taken down, de-taped and rolled up, seeds to be separated and chairs, tables, screens and other vulnerable equipment to be repaired and put back in some semblance of their former condition and patterns. There may also be mess outside any room which has been a centre of activity.

With minimal instruction, this can be done by volunteers. A final celebration of SOSOTEC and cooperation.

21 Make your own collection

Answers to 'Whose reality? Teasers':

- Monkeys roosting in the trees ate crops. Thickets of dense branching in the tamarind trees thwarted those who tried to drive the monkeys away by throwing or shooting with catapults.
- Causing trouble with neighbours. As a result goats had been banned from the village.
- The degree to which it would send the child to sleep. Top scorers for this were mother's milk and gruel, each with five out of five.
- The degree to which the fodder would precipitate oestrus (coming on heat) in cows.
- The second priority was places where they could wash in private, and the third that measures should be taken about dowry.
- They could think of no improvement!
- The half coconut shells were tied over their muzzles when necessary to stop them eating crops they were passing through (source: Anindo Banerjee).
- The women who threw stones had no toilets and had to defecate in the open during the hours of darkness.

- '… funerals'. The area had a high death rate (especially AIDS-related) and nearly every day there was a funeral. The poorest people attended every funeral and moved from one to another, so that they could get some food to eat. (From the field notes of Mary Simasuku, in Shah et al, 1999, p48.)

21 Ideas and Options for Analysis and Feedback

These 21 tips and options address two questions:

A Is this something people can think through and work out for themselves?

We can ask this question again, *and again*, **and again and AGAIN**. Have our own experiences of being 'taught' conditioned us to 'teach' in turn? It is quite amazing how often formal teaching is not needed for learning. There is so much people can think of and analyse for themselves without having to be lectured to or taught. With a little encouragement, they can reflect, recollect, note, diagram, make lists, categorize, see connections – in short, do their own analysis and generate their own insights. Often they do not know they can. They believe they cannot. When teachers and trainers also believe they cannot, a sad syndrome of lack of confidence, lack of encouragement and lack of occasion sustains a myth of incapacity. Top-down 'I know, they are ignorant' mindsets and behaviours in teachers, trainers and facilitators are self-validating.

'We don't know how to map.'

'They don't know how to map.'

'Of course they don't. What do you expect? They're illiterate, uneducated, too young, too old...'[1]

Frequently this is nonsense. Most people can do for themselves much more than their seniors and superiors suppose. One of the sayings in PRA is 'They Can Do It'. When 'uppers' show confidence in the belief that 'lowers' can do something, often, so often, lowers discover for themselves that they can. For this the uppers have to hold back. They must not teach. At most they convene, initiate and catalyse. They

---

1 A partial exception is highly educated intellectuals who have been so damaged by their life experiences, self-images and self-consciousness that they have lost the freedom to fool about and create. Dr Seuss was right to say that 'adults are obsolete children'. We are all obsolete to different degrees. But the premature senility of some inhibited intellectuals is a disabling personal tragedy. The radical rehabilitation they deserve is usually ruled out by their inability to recognize that they need it.

provide occasions, contexts and encouragement. If they start by holding a stick, they quickly hand it over.

When people do their own analysis, they can:

- learn from the process;
- own the outcome;
- gain confidence;
- develop their capabilities;
- discover things for themselves;
- show things we did not know or did not know to ask;
- show one another things they did not know.

B How best can ideas, insights and information be fed back, shown and shared?

There is no one 'best way'; rather there is a struggle to find good ways of doing this, context by context. Words are the most obvious, but there is a wider repertoire of means and media. Those given below are simply a sample. There are surely many more. There is plenty of space for creativity. Discover your own.

For clarity, analysis and feedback are presented below separately. In practice, they are often an intermingled flow, combining and overlapping in many ways. All of which adds to choice, variety and fun with scope for improvising and inventing.

Contents

POWER AND PROCESS

In many participatory processes there is a progressive shift of power, with a sequence from control to empowerment, from plenary to individual or group, from centred to dispersed. Then there may be a return to the centre for feedback, by which time relationships have changed. Such sequences can be fulfilling and fun. They can also lighten the burden on the facilitator.

One good sequence is:

- plenary briefing;
- individual reflection and noting;
- small group sharing and discussion;
- groups feedback to plenary;
- plenary discussion (with or without buzzes).

1 Disempower yourself

Especially in plenaries, trainers, teachers and facilitators tend to dominate and lead. Most of us like talking to groups. We lecture. We facipulate. We stand while others sit. There is a board, screen and projector which indicate a spatial focus of authority and control where we stand or sit. There is a table or lectern between us and 'them'.

Most of us talk too much, dominate too much, control too much. We need to learn to talk less, to dominate less, to control less. The challenge is to 'walk the non-talk', to shut up and to empower and trust others. Facilitating others' analysis means disempowering ourselves, handing over the stick, leading by withdrawing. It can mean what Latin Americans call 'suffering the silence', waiting while others think before they talk and act, controlling our sense of obligation to fill silence with speech.

To do this we can:

- decentre – move away from the spatial focus of authority;
- sit down;
- shut up;
- initiate self-organizing processes;
- hand over to a participant;
- refer questions back to groups;
- ask for others' contributions;
- start individual reflection, buzzes or small groups;
- go away (one of the hardest lessons is to know when not to be there).

We can ask ourselves: who facilitates? Volunteer facilitators can handle a feedback session, for example. When participants facilitate and we take back seats:

- the rhythm changes;
- it often goes better (well, that is my experience);
- ownership is spread;
- we get a rest.

Try it, and be surprised.

2 Empower individuals

Start by asking each person to reflect and note or list for themselves, without discussing with others. This starts everyone thinking and realizing that they know something already about a subject. The notes and lists give each person something to share. This leads well into group discussions which are more democratic because each person has a note of things to say.

Tip

• Insist on silence during individual reflection and noting.

3 Empower groups

Give tasks to groups. There are many sorts and sizes of groups [see **11**]. Much of the best analysis seems to take place in small groups of, say, three to five members. Some pros and cons of groups are:

Pros

• People participate, talk, share and learn by talking and sharing.
• More knowledge is on tap.
• Cross-checking and confidence building take place.
• Synergy and enthusiasm are generated.
• Group analysis often goes beyond what one person could achieve.
• Those with special knowledge share it with others.

Cons

• One or two people may dominate.
• Discussions can go off at a tangent.
• A rapporteur may give unrepresentative views.
• Difficult in a lecture theatre.

Tips and options

• [See **11** and **19**].
• Go for mapping and diagramming [see 7 below]. Maps and diagrams can generate group-visual synergy:[2] motivation mounts, and enthusiastic activity takes off in thinking, remembering, showing and cross-checking.
• When some know more, others less, of a topic, ask them to pair off or form small groups. Those knowing more share with those knowing less.

2 See Chambers, 1997b, pp159–60.

SOME OPTIONS FOR PARTICIPATORY ANALYSIS

Institutions for training and teaching often get stuck in ruts of a narrow repertoire of media and methods. Mainly these are for teaching, for transmitting information. Some are largely verbal, some a mix of verbal and audio-visual. Some are peculiar to a subject, discipline or profession.

To enable people to do their own thinking and analysis, there are many methods, sequences and combinations available, some old and some new. Items 4–12 present some of these.

4 Talking

Talking is the overvalued default mode. Of course we communicate much of the time through words. They are almost always used as some part of analysis. And they have many advantages. But language organized in sentences is a primitive means for analysing complexity:

- The spoken word is transient.
- The subject-verb-object structure of sentences in many languages restricts the range of relationships that can be expressed.
- The mind retains only a fraction of what has been written or said.
- When we are talking, some people tend to dominate, others to withdraw.
- What is said and shared is influenced by social relationships, and by speakers choosing and moulding what they say to fit the context.

It is striking that when thinking hard and creatively, we tend to abandon sentences and use disjointed words and diagrams. Words gain in power and utility when combined with other media and methods.

Tips and options

[See other 21s especially **16** and **19**.]

5 Listing and combining

Active analysis and sharing in a short sequence. Groups list points or items on sheets of paper using coloured pens (one colour per group). Stop when the lists are long enough. Groups swap pens to a different colour. Each group in turn shouts out one item. Others tick it if they have it; if not, they write it in with the different coloured pen. At the end, all should have the same full list.

Examples of lists are:

- dimensions of a good quality of life;
- dimensions of a bad quality of life;
- uppers and lowers;
- advantages of ground and paper in mapping.

Tips and options

- Shout and copy. In sharing, ask one person from each group to stand up, one to choose their next item to contribute and one to write. Those standing then shout out loud in turn, allowing time for the writing by other groups. (This is lively, regulates itself and allows you a breather.)
- Invite one group to share its whole list first, and then others to add what has not been covered (less noisy and quicker but less participatory).
- Ask for volunteers to make a consolidated list later and post it up. This then represents a collective effort and does not take up much wall space.
- Use in the sequence: (1) Form random groups, for example, through 'Number clumps' or 'Jungle' [see **11**:2 and **11**:4]; (2) Fill in flip charts on the ground, and then; (3) Share and combine.
- Individuals briefly make their own lists. Move into groups quickly before the lists are long. (Long lists can gum up a group and inhibit group brainstorming.)

6 Card writing and sorting

A powerful and versatile technique, often excellent as part of a participatory sequence. Individuals or small groups write on cards. These are thrown on the ground. Participants sort the cards into categories. These are then stuck up on a wall to be more visible.

Applications

- Identifying the agenda for a workshop [see **5**:20].
- Sorting and analysing large quantities of qualitative data. Used in Participatory Poverty Assessments in South Africa and Tanzania, and in the Community Empowerment Zones programme in the US, in both Tanzania and the US with some 800 cards.

CARD WRITING AND SORTING

- Identifying and analysing categories such as dimensions of poverty.
- Listing from brainstorms.

Tips and options

- Use large pens, large or capital letters and few words.
- Similar cards can be piled or laid in a line. The number of cards then shows frequency of mention.
- When cards are being sorted into categories, listen and watch for emerging categories and write them boldly on new cards (making them stand out in a new colour ink, and/or on cards of a different colour, size or shape).
- To put the cards on a wall either:
  - stick them individually (tiresome);

- stick them on a length of masking tape, sticky side outwards, and hang them up;
- stick them on a sheet that has been sprayed with adhesive – the cards can then be placed and repositioned easily; or
- spray the back of each card and stick it on paper, material or wall.
- If a workshop is to divide into groups, choose topics or clusters of topics for groups so that each group has a similar number of cards. These will usually attract those who wrote the cards. Numbers in the groups will then be roughly equivalent.
- Cards can be scored for different criteria (see 8 below).
- On the ground participants turn over or make a mark on cards they disagree with or want discussed. Those not turned over or marked are taken as agreed, and those turned over or marked are debated.

Sources: For sequences with card sorting on the ground see Chambers, 1997a and Attwood and Gaventa, 1998.

7 Participatory visuals and tangibles: mapping, modelling, matrices and diagramming

Effective and widely applicable means to express and analyse complexity in ways that words alone cannot. These are only a short selection of many PRA or PLA methods. For a practical guide to visual methods, see *Embracing Participation in Development: Wisdom from the Field* [**21**:4, Part 3].

Participatory mapping and modelling are popular and widespread. Participants draw, elaborate on and analyse their own maps or models. These can represent anything with a spatial dimension – social maps showing people and their types; health maps – people, resources and services; mobility maps – where people go for services; vulnerability maps – dangerous places; defecation maps – where people go to go; maps of farms or gardens or trees; maps for buildings (youth design a youth club, children a house and so on); and models for the environment – amenities in inner cities, rural watersheds, and so on.

Matrices are versatile templates for analysis. One strong application is *matrix scoring*. Items to be compared are listed across the top of a sheet and criteria for comparing them down the side. A matrix is drawn. The boxes are then scored using seeds, stones or counters. Scoring out of five or ten in each box is common. In scoring a matrix, consensus is usually better than voting, which gives more influence to those who vote last, since they can see earlier votes. Free scoring (any number in any box) is better than trained professionals may suppose. Adding up is problematical (see Maxwell and Bart, 1995 and Fielding and Riley, 2000).

Diagrams take many forms. Timelines lay out historical sequences. Causal linkages are shown by arranging cards or symbols and connecting them with lines and arrows. For Venn (chapati in South Asia, tortilla in Latin America, dumpling in Jamaica, etc) diagrams, use circular papers or stones of different sizes arranged to express the importance, quality and relationships of different institutions or people. Seasonality and trend diagrams show changes sequentially over time. Flow diagrams show sequence in a process. And so on.

Tips and options

- Remember that with visuals, using the ground first and then paper second is often a good sequence.
- Ask participants to choose, or find yourself, a suitable space for the activity.
- Be sparing in instructions. Allow for creativity.
- Encourage the use of local materials. It is also useful to have basic materials available such as chalks for the ground, pens, paper and seeds.
- 'Interview' the visual. This means asking questions and probing the meanings of what has been shown.
- Encourage additions and changes and use of the visual for reference.
- Stick up a visual on which participants mark details. Examples:
  - where you come from or where you know about, on a map;
  - the best time for poor women to meet, on a 24-hour diagram;
  - the most difficult times of year, on a seasonal calendar.

This can be quick and participatory, and clear and easy to discuss. The map or diagram remains as a reminder or agenda.

For participatory applications of modelling for planning see *The Power in Our Hands* (Gibson, 1996).

8 Ranking and scoring

A rich range of methods. Items, options or agendas are identified and variously counted, estimated, scored or ranked. Ranking and scoring are often parts of sequences and take many forms. Among the most common and effective are:

Ranking by sorting cards or pieces of paper on the ground or on a table. The items can originate from group brainstorming, or they can be preset and provided by you. Examples are the ranking for relative status of different professions or different university departments. Ranking can also be through relative scores.

Tip

After groups have ranked items, have a walk around and debate where there are differences.

Scoring by allocating seeds or stickers to items, or by making marks against them. One way is to allocate a fixed number of seeds, stickers or marks (say five or seven, or whatever) to each person. They then distribute these between items.

Tips

- Minimize queues to place seeds, stickers or marks by running the activity into a break and/or by spreading out or duplicating the cards or lists of items.

- If two or more lists are needed, have them compiled at the same time. (For example, two lists were prepared simultaneously from a brainstorming of words used in development. One was then scored for importance, and the other for the degree of hypocrisy with which the words were used.)
- Clarify how the marks can be given – whether there is a maximum for one item, or only one per item, or whether any number within the personal limit can be allocated to a single item.
- Marks can be added and new ranked lists prepared, but the original messy lists with participants' marks tend to have greater immediacy, impact and ownership.

9 Drawing

Creative and fun. Individuals or groups draw to represent their views of something. This can be, for example, a self-portrait (in introductions), or a concept like 'participation', 'trust' or 'empowerment'. These are then displayed, explained and discussed.

Some facilitators hesitate to use drawing, perhaps partly because there is a need to 'suffer the silence' while participants are puzzling what and how to draw. But drawing can be a powerful means of self-expression and of showing the person drawing how they see something; and their view of it evolves as they make it more explicit.

Tips

- Be daring. Despite early inhibitions and difficulties, it is astonishing what people find they can do.
- A playful energizer before drawing can help.

10 Acting: role plays and theatre

A still undervalued medium for exploring, analysis, feedback and communicating. Often memorable. Role plays and theatre open up wonderful scope across the whole range of learning, analysis and exploring realities and implications. In role plays and theatre there is a special licence: the unsayable can be said; the hidden can be revealed; power can be mocked and made to laugh at itself. By acting out situations, people can uncover and discover aspects otherwise overlooked or unknown.

Tips

- Allow enough time. Preparation, performance and discussion tend to take longer than expected.
- Discuss after a performance. Much may come out.

11 Stand, see, debate and move

Lively, versatile and engaging ways to make every-one think and take a position, making differences visible. Tends to encourage humour and discourage animosity.

Identify differences of opinion or judgement (about objectives, proposals, values, preferences, organizations, ways of doing things ...). Mark these out spatially – written on the ground, posted on flip charts or simply shouted out; or if the differences are polar dimensions, point out the extreme ends. Participants then move to the position that best expresses their view or judge-ment. Everyone can then see the range of differences, and who is where. Discussion and debate follow.

STAND, SEE AND DEBATE

One form is Yes, Yes But, No But, No. Choose a contro-versial statement. Space out four stations (Yes, Yes But, No But, No) along a wall. Ask everyone to reflect first and then go to the station that best fits their view. Facilitate argument and persuasion, perhaps starting with a minority view. People move as their views change.

Tips and options

* Encourage movement between positions.
* If eventual consensus is sought on a Yes, Yes But, No But, No statement, invite suggestions for changing its wording.

Sources: include Binoy Acharya (Ahmedabad 1998) for Yes, Yes But, No But, No, and Jethro Pettit and Garett Pratt for other applications.

12 Participatory Powerpoint

A relatively quick, democratic and efficient way of drafting and modifying text, superior to any alternative I know. Well used, it is highly participatory and can move rapidly to consensus. Avoids the common defect of Powerpoint of too much infor-mation presented too fast.

Arrange seating so that all can comfortably face and see the screen. One person controls the Powerpoint and makes entries on the basis of the discussion. Points or text being considered but not yet agreed are highlighted. Everyone can see what is being discussed and agreed. The final text can be printed out for participants.

Tips

* The Powerpoint can be used by a chairperson or perhaps better by someone chosen for their knowledge, sensitivity and computer competence. Whoever is entering the Powerpoint needs to be skilled and alert, and to enter suggestions

as they are being made, and not wait until there is consensus. This saves a lot of time.

- A good seating arrangement is a hollow square or U, with the computer in the centre and the screen at the open end.
- Ensure a reliable electricity supply or batteries, and be prepared for something to go wrong with some part of the system.

Sources: Andrea Cornwall, John Gaventa and the Millennium Ecosystem Assessment Second Design Workshop, Capetown, October 2001

SOME OPTIONS FOR FEEDBACK

After small group analysis there is often feedback and sharing ('reporting back') to plenary. This can take many forms. One is written reports. The short repertoire here is a selection of verbal and visual techniques.

13 Speaking

Spoken feedback is natural and familiar. This can be by a rapporteur from each group. The fashion for flip charts or transparencies has led to neglect of the virtues of simple speech. It avoids the delays and distractions of other methods. And what people say is often more lively than what they write.

Tips and options

- Give a time limit.
- Invite others from each group to supplement or correct.
- *Panel bullets* is a good option. Rapporteurs form a panel. Each in turn makes one bullet point only, not repeating anything already said. This continues until no panel member has anything more to contribute. This:
  - minimizes repetitions;
  - prevents rambling;
  - maintains interest among listeners;
  - makes it easy to record points;
  - saves time.

Source: Jacqueline Kabambe

14 Flip charts

A standard medium for feedback from group discussions. For many facilitators, trainers and teachers, flip charts are *the* medium and means for feedback. They are easily understood, and are often familiar to participants. They concentrate the minds of groups who know that an output is expected, and will be seen by others. They leave a permanent record which can stay on view and be written up later. Their items can also be scored (see 8 above).

Flip charts can be filled and presented in many ways. Many facilitators use only one or two. But there are at least six options:

You elicit and write

You elicit in plenary. Ask for items and write up a chart as you go. Groups or individuals can give responses in turn. You control the words used and what is recorded because you are writing it up. At the end there is one chart with the idiosyncratic obscurity or clarity, as the case may be, of your writing.

Volunteers elicit

One or more volunteers elicit and write up responses in plenary. This can work well. The volunteers often write better than you (speaking personally).

Tip

For lists of paired items, two volunteers write up simultaneously, one on either side of the chart. For example, for listing pairs of uppers and lowers, called out by participants, one writes in the uppers and the other the lowers.

Group rapporteurs write and present

Group rapporteurs write on flip charts. One or more rapporteurs present these to the plenary. Someone chairs the process.

Tips

- Too many groups presenting is tedious. Three to five is usually enough.
- Ask groups to pick a rapporteur before they start.
- Encourage presenters to face the audience, not the flip chart.
- After a presentation ask others from the group if they wish to add anything.
- The chair may need to be strict about time; or each group can time its successor.
- Try to get through any weak report early, and keep the best report for last.

Groups write and post up on a wall

Charts can then be presented in turn, or simply studied and commented on. This is good for participation and movement if everyone stands up and walks around but tends to:

- use a lot of wall space;
- take a long time;
- show a confusing mass of points, and be difficult to consolidate. Sometimes there is simply too much to take in, and people wander off and start other conversations.

Tips and options

- Consolidate. Ask volunteers to make one consolidated list to replace more numerous charts.

- When flip charts have been posted up, participants use coloured pens to mark points of agreement and disagreement which can then be debated.

Send to write up

After discussions, each group sends a representative to write up on one or more centrally placed flip chart sheets. This is good for movement but is:

- open to repetition and difficulty aggregating;
- liable to illegible scribbles;
- subject to delays with queuing;
- a passive time/nice break and rest for those not writing up.

Send to a volunteer who writes up

This is the fastest effective sequence for consolidating feedback from groups that are making lists, for example of Dos and Don'ts. It is lively and produces a quick, visible list that can also be immediately scored.

- Break into groups. Each group brainstorms.
- A volunteer with flip chart and pen is ready to record contributions. (For two lists, as with Dos and Don'ts, have a separate volunteer and flip chart for each.)
- As groups generate ideas they send members to give them to the volunteer(s) while the rest continue to brainstorm.
- The volunteers record the lists and add a tick when the same item is repeated.

Tips and options

- Encourage groups to make contributions soon after starting to discuss. This reduces queuing later.
- With two or more lists, avoid congestion by placing the flip charts well apart (eg at opposite ends of the room).
- Run the activity into a break so that groups can finish at different times and the break can be used to read, reflect and consolidate.

15 Overhead transparencies

Overhead projector transparencies have been a popular way to report back. If a photocopier is available and working, and if anyone remembers, they can be copied and given to participants.

In practice they are vulnerable to:

- too much information presented too fast;
- illegibility – longhand, or writing too small;
- poor placement on the screen (reversed, upside down or too big);
- the reporter reads out slowly his/her(or someone else's writing) when the audience's eyes and minds are travelling faster;

- distraction by striptease (shifting a masking sheet to show more and more until the sheet falls off, revealing all);
- divided attention between what is said and what is seen;
- rushed attempts to copy down what is being shown which impedes listening and leaves incomplete notes when the transparency is whisked away;
- photocopies promised but not delivered;
- electricity failure and bulb blow out.

Tips and options (for rapporteurs)

- Go to the back beforehand to check visibility.
- Use diagrams where you can.
- Write few words, to capture only major points or headings.
- Speak to headings.
- Do not read out.
- Leave each transparency up for some time.
- Hand out copies *in advance* so that people can take notes and/or add amendments (but beware! This can seriously distract attention).

16 Visuals and tangibles

Good for showing complex relationships quickly and clearly, and concentrating attention. Visuals and tangibles can be photocopied handouts, diagrams, collections of cards, scored matrices, and the like. They can save much time. The more they show, the less needs to be said. Diagrams drawn on paper can also be kept for later analysis.

Tip

To see visuals laid out on the ground it may help if those in front sit and those at the back stand on chairs.

17 Reporting by acting

Fun, focuses attention, and fabulous for feedback that is critical or on sensitive subjects. Reporting through theatre or role playing can be powerful (see 10 above).

One form is feedback through a conversation in front of the whole group. The conversation can take several forms – a debate presenting different views (not necessarily held by the presenters), a review of what was discussed in a group, or simply sharing information.

REPORT BY ACTING

Source: Sam Musa and Kaliba Songhore, Entebbe, May 1998

18 Combinations and sequences

Modes of analysis and feedback are often stronger when combined and sequenced. Combinations and sequences are myriad, with enormous scope for improvisation and inventiveness. For example, drawing and acting can fit and follow other modes in many ways. Some of the more common combinations involve visuals and tangibles. Some examples are when participants, individually or in groups:

- Brainstorm, sort and rank or score. Items or points are brainstormed on to cards, which are then sorted and ranked or scored for one or more criteria or characteristics (see 8 above). Excellent for reflection by participants and for their ownership.
- Draw and add to maps and then enter on them marks, linkages, estimates, scores and/or preferences. (Farmers at Karatina in Kenya drew farm maps elaborated with lines representing nutrient flows which were then scored for importance. They also diagrammed for seasonality and listed and matrix scored the types of organic matter that went into compost pits.)
- Number the linking lines and arrows on causal-linkage diagrams and then list actions to deal with them, one by one.
- Use matrix scoring to compare institutions identified in Venn diagramming.
- Go from a time line to a historical matrix showing changes in dimensions, activities, populations and so on.

WHAT AND WHERE?

19 Transient images on screens

Overhead projector transparencies, slides and Powerpoint need screens, white walls or stretched sheets.

Beware. Things shown on screens are transient. Projections of slides look bleached if there is sunlight in a room. And frightful fates lurk for those who rely on machines and electricity [see **9**:8–12].

Tips and options

- Decentre by putting a screen somewhere other than at the 'head' of the room.
- Use a screen as extra wall space for wall posters (with masking tape, not Blu Tack).
- Most screens respond to love and patience. They are best angled forward to be at right angles to the aim of a projector. For this, some movable screens have a notched arm at the top of the vertical support. This clever device can collapse catastrophically, cutting and bruising and leaving bent bits of metal . Have to hand masking tape for the screen's repairs and Band-aid for yours.
- If there is a small detail on a slide or transparency, invite everyone to get up and come close to look. A good wake-up for dozy dreamers.
- If something is important, show it twice. It is then more likely to be remembered.

20 Durable displays on walls

Displays on walls have advantages:
- Durability, unless they fall down. They can be studied and copied at will.
- Reinforcement. Seen several times, they make a deeper impression.
- Flexibility. They can be referred to at any time (without that embarrassing hunt for the missing overhead transparency).
- Movement. They allow and encourage movement during a session.
- Decentring. They disperse spatial authority.

But:

- Wall charts are heavy to carry around.
- They do often fall down.
- You may not change and update them as much as you should (*mea culpa*).
- They take time to put up, take down, and roll up.

Still, on balance, they have much to recommend them.

Tips and options

- Be selective. Too many displays can be overkill.
- Carry charts around as a roll. Have a suitcase in which they fit.
- Go round and press down the ends of masking tape. These tend to curl, leading to collapse.
- Exercise zero tolerance when charts fall down. However badly prepared or grotty they are, keep them up in place. Put extra lengths of tape on whichever of the wall or the chart the tape has peeled off.
- With plenty of wall space, develop a sequence of charts representing the subjects covered and the outputs, day by day, of a workshop. This helps in a walk around for final evaluation [see **7**].
- When taking charts down, do first aid (on the charts) with used bits of masking tape.
- Ensure that all masking tape has been bent back or removed before rolling charts up. Otherwise carnage ensues when they are next unrolled.

21 Invent, analyse and share your own

21 Ways to Help Each Other Learn

Teaching is not the same as learning. This is not about 'normal' teaching. This is about what teaching should be – helping each other to learn.

Figures about learning and remembering cited by sourcebooks and manuals, though dubious, do provoke reflection. For example:

> Tests have shown that people remember:
> 20% of what they Hear
> 40% of what the Hear and See
> and 80% of what They Discover For Themselves
> *Source: Teaching for Transformation: Vol 1* [see **21**:9, p103]

> HOW WE LEARN
> 1% through taste
> 2% through touch
> 3% through smell
> 11% through hearing
> 83% through sight

REMEMBER

> WHAT WE REMEMBER
> 10% of what we read
> 20% of what we hear
> 30% of what we see
> 50% of what we see and hear
> 80% of what we say
> 90% of what we say and do
> *Source: Visualisation in Participatory Programmes*
> [see **21**:14, piv]

Most learning is more than just remembering. Words that describe deeper learning include personal development, personal growth, internalization and self-realization.

Learning occurs in many ways and combinations of ways. 21 propositions or principles underpin, and can be inferred from, the 21 learning activities that follow. The propositions or principles are:

- People know more than they realize they know.
- People can do more than they think they can do.
- Groups know more than individuals.
- Groups can find out more than individuals.
- We learn by thinking things out for ourselves.
- We learn through thinking things out with others.
- We learn through debate and discussion.
- We learn through experiment.
- We learn through play and fun.
- We learn through mixes of activity, topic and movement.
- We learn by doing and through experience.
- We learn through embracing error.
- We learn through recollection.
- We learn through reflection.
- We learn by talking.
- We learn by helping others learn ('learning by teaching and training').
- We learn better from peers than from teachers.
- We learn by doubting.
- We learn by breaking rules.
- We learn by working out our own ways of doing things, with our own pragmatic principles.
- We learn from lists shorter than 21.

Contents

1 List and share

For starting with what people know. On many subjects, people already know something. Ask them to make lists from their own knowledge, experience, imagination and reflection.

Lists can be individual to begin with. This makes everyone think. It can give confidence to those who otherwise would hold back. Individual lists can then be shared, consolidated and added to in small groups. Or listing can take place straight away through brainstorming in small groups.

Examples of what people can list on their own

- Uppers and lowers (pairs in which one is dominant, the other subordinate).
- Advantages of ground or paper for mapping and diagramming.
- Dimensions of wellbeing.
- Dimensions of deprivation.
- Bad effects of the tropical rainy season on poor people.
- How to deal with dominators.
- Dos and don'ts (for facilitating groups, establishing rapport, etc).

2 Compile and collate

For drawing together and discussing lists, and adding to them. This can follow on from individual and small group analysis.

Individuals or groups think, list and write items on cards, with a separate card for each item. They arrange the cards on the ground, clustering them by category. When so organized, they stick them up on a wall. Discuss the outcome. You or others can add any categories or points missed or thought of later.

COMPILE AND COLLATE

Examples

See 1 above. To illustrate, two others are:

- correlates of high and low professional status;
- reasons why a poor family did not take their sick child to the clinic in the tropical wet season, when they would have in the dry season.

Tips and options

- Manage time with parallel activities – listing, sorting and sticking up can go on simultaneously.
- Write a bold heading to label each column as it emerges on the ground.
- Display on the wall using sticky material, sticky spray, or with each column of cards on a vertical length of masking tape.
- Have your own checklist in case points are left out.
- Take time over the discussion. Invite reflection on why some points were more obvious and others less so. Ask groups to discuss what they contributed and what they missed, and why.
- Leave up on the wall for the rest of the session.

3 Carousel

For active learning with movement. Topics for learning activities are identified, either by participants, or by you. The activity can be something to study, something to learn, a problem to solve, analysing a problem, a colleague sharing experience and so on. Each topic has a resource person (facilitator, teacher or participant). Each of these has a station – a separate space or room. A time limit is set for each round of activity. Divide into equal groups, one group to each station. Rotate the groups at intervals, while the resource persons stay put and repeat.

Tips

- The movement and diverse activities make this good for late morning and the afternoon 'graveyard session'.
- Groups can have any number of members.
- Anything between five and 30 minutes can be a good length for each activity.
- Two–five stations is a usual range.
- Site the stations for ease of synchronization and movement between them.
- Make sure station facilitators know where groups should go next and tell departing groups clearly where to go! (Once a group goes to the wrong place it is tricky to put things right again. When a group went to the wrong station in Kyrgyzstan, chaos was compounded by muddled attempts to correct it.)

4 Peer circus

A carousel or circus in which peers do the teaching or facilitation. Topics are identified. Participants then volunteer for or are allocated topics to study and prepare to 'teach'.
Proceed as for carousel.

Tips and options

- Arrange a separate session for the peers who did the teaching to teach each other. Otherwise they will miss out.
- Allow slightly longer for the first round. Presenters tend to be able to speed up as they gain experience.

See also Tips under Carousel

5 The teaching–learning wheel

For understanding, analysing and memorizing a short text, diagrams or illustrative photographs. Extraordinarily effective for dull or not-so-dull material, but so unconventional that I doubt whether it will ever be adopted widely. Sad. Do prove me wrong.

Arrange tables in a circle, one table to two people. Put a different section of the text, or a different diagram or photograph, on each table. If it is text or diagram, have enough copies for all participants.

Two participants sit at each table and study, discuss and learn the subject matter. Text can be memorized if desired. One person then stays while the other moves on clockwise to the next table. Those who moved are taught or explained to by those who stayed. In the next round, those who stayed the first time move anticlockwise, and those who moved stay as teachers or explainers. Continue alternating movements like this until complete. So each participant alternates moving and staying. For any one person, moves are always in the same direction. Thus it is:

1   Pairs discuss and familiarize.
2   One stays to explain. The other moves clockwise and is explained to.
3   Those who stayed in round two move anticlockwise. Those who moved stay and explain.
4   Those who stayed in round three move clockwise. Those who moved stay and explain and so on.

Tips and option

•   Explain carefully who moves which way when.
•   The first session needs more time than later ones.
•   Walk around during the first session, explain detail and deal with questions.
•   With larger numbers, have either two or more circles of pairs, or have pairs or threes teaching and moving together instead of individuals.

6 Merry-go-round

A lively method for covering much material in a short time. Suitable for diagrams or short texts. Once set up it frees you to wander around.

I have found this works well with diagrams illustrating aspects of tropical seasonality.

MERRY-GO-ROUND

1   Select diagrams or texts. Make enough copies for each participant.
2   Arrange tables separately in a circle. Number the tables. Put all the copies of one diagram or text on each table.
3   Form roughly equal-sized groups, one at each table.
4   Invite each group to study the diagram or text on their table and understand it. Walk around and explain where necessary.
5   Each group moves on. One person remains to explain the diagram or text to the next group.

6   At the next move, someone else stays to explain.
7   Continue until finished.

Tips

*   It is neat if the group is a square number (eg 16 is four groups of four persons at four tables, 25 is five groups of five persons at five tables, or 36 is six groups of six persons at six tables). Then each person stays behind once. But it works out all right with any numbers. The main difference is that, with numbers that are not squares, some do not have the chance to be an explainer.
*   One or two tables may need help. Be alert and available.
*   Check that everyone has a full set of the texts or diagrams at the end.

7 Pairing cards

For analysing contrasted pairs of characteristics.

1   List the contrasted pairs and write on separate (ie one for each item in a pair) cards or slips of paper. Make up as many sets, each set shuffled, as there will be groups of analysts.
2   Hand out a set to each group and invite them to sort them into contrasted pairs, arranged in a column.
3   All walk around and see what others have done, debate and discuss.
4   Plenary summation and discussion.

Examples

*   The contrasting characteristics of blueprint and process approaches in development.
*   The world-views and realities of professionals and poor people or any other two paradigms.

Tips and options

*   Sorting can be on tables or on the floor.
*   Do not rush the discussion.
*   Have a handout at the end which summarizes the pairs.
*   At the end ask groups to collect their slips or cards together ready for another time (otherwise it can take ages to do it yourself).

8 Case study comparisons

Brilliant for comparative analysis of written case studies. A powerful sequence for remembering, analysis and learning. Having to present a case study to someone else in a small group is a fine incentive without the public exposure of a larger group.

Don't be put off because this looks complicated. It is well worth the trouble. Feedback has been enthusiastic.

1   Form groups of three.
2   Give each group two copies of each of three case studies (total six).
3   Each group member receives two case studies but not the third.
4   Each member studies one in detail and reads the second to have some familiarity with it. (This is often assigned as an overnight task.)
5   Groups meet. Each member in turn presents and explains the case study they have examined in detail to the group member who has not seen it. The third member who has read the case presented is able to comment and supplement.
6   Repeat until each has done each task and all three cases have been presented.

Examples

- Case studies of the lives of poor people.
- Case studies of the use of a procedure or process.
- Case studies of a type of project.

Tips

- Warn in advance about the time required, and that this is a commitment to colleagues in a small group.
- If the cases are rich, allow plenty of time for plenary sharing and discussion at the end.
- This combines well with dimension analysis (see below).

9 Dimension analysis of case studies

For cross-cutting analysis of case studies. Powerful when combined with 8 above. Identify cross-cutting dimensions that can apply to the cases (eg vulnerability, sustainability, coping with crisis, participation). Invite volunteers or allocate these so that each dimension has a champion analyst, and so that each dimension is covered in each group, as in 8 above.

Each champion examines the cases, asks questions and collects relevant insights. These can be shared later in plenary.

Tips and option

- When combined with case study presentations, cross-cutting groups of champions can meet together (eg those concerned with vulnerability together, those concerned with sustainability together, etc). Then one person can present to plenary for the group of champions.

10 Card listing and sequencing

Good for analysis and presentation of change. Invite participants to write on cards aspects of something which has changed over time. These can be related to concepts, commonly used words, policies, experiences and so on. The cards are sorted and sequenced on the ground or wall, and then discussed.

Examples

- words, concepts, dominant theories
- fashions
- authors, novels
- foods

Tips

- Note any obvious gaps and add cards for these.
- Allow enough time for reflection.
- Summarize. Otherwise the many cards can look confusing.

11 Interrogate

Good for encouraging active investigation. One person prepares a subject, or already knows about it, or has relevant experience. Others ask questions. The 'expert' replies, but only to questions asked. This provokes questioners into thinking about what to ask.

INTERROGATE

Tips and options

- Interrogation can be based on a paper, article or book written by the 'expert' (a splendid way of varying the standard format of presentation followed by questions and discussion).
- Participants or students can be the experts; for example, study-ing a text or subject overnight, or something they have experienced or know about anyway.
- At the end, the 'expert' can tell the questioners what they failed to ask about.

12 One-pagers

Simple, easy and effective. Hand out a one-pager, either text, diagram, drawing or photograph. Ask for, say, five minutes of individual reflection, followed by small group sharing and discussion followed by plenary.

Tip

- If the diagram or drawing is complicated or difficult, show it first with an overhead projector and explain it. This can save much time and confusion.

13 Anonymous peer evaluation

For learning from critical analysis and frank evaluation. A versatile method which engages thought and reflection. Facilitate an activity which leads to a personal map, drawing, diagram or statement on a piece of paper. These are passed around and commented on by others in writing. Those commenting do not know whose paper it is. Originators receive back their papers with anonymous comments. The comments tend to be franker than they might be face-to-face.

Examples

- The layout of your office (a map).
- What does participation look like? (a drawing).
- What are the effects of dominating behaviour? (a diagram).
- What is development? (a statement).

Options and tips

- Emphasize that the purpose is to learn from thinking about and commenting on what others have done, and from their comments on one's own output.
- Encourage constructive comments.
- Judge whether anonymity is needed. It may or may not be.
- To assure anonymity with small numbers, shuffle the papers before starting evaluation.
- With larger numbers, sit in groups (say four–eight in a group, depending on how many comments are sought), and swap papers between groups, returning them after comments.

14 Send on an insight

For participatory learning and selective sharing. Groups discuss a topic. They then select an insight, reflection or finding to share with others. Each then sends a messenger to the next group to pass it on. This allows more discussion and interaction than occurs with presentations direct to plenary.

Options

- This can be repeated several times, sending on different messengers.
- Messengers can go on again and share in other groups.
- Messengers can collect reactions and responses, and finally report these to plenary. (This allows messengers to learn from each other and also reinforces learning and insights for others.)

15 Seek answers

For involving all participants in active thinking and talking about key questions or issues. Divide into three roughly equal groups (A, B and C). Each group identifies or is given a key question. The questions are written up for all to see.

Form new groups of three, each with one person from A, one from B and one from C. In each of these new groups, A asks B and C the A question. Then B asks C and A the B question. Finally C asks A and B the C question. The As, Bs and Cs then meet again in their original groups and compare and collate the responses they received.

The As, Bs and Cs then present in turn to the whole group.

Options

• Can also be done with two groups, and with encounters which are one to one, or two to two. Or with four groups. But three is probably the best number.

16 Ranking

For ranking things when there is something to learn from the rankings.

1 Hand out identical sets of prepared slips to teams, or ask them to write items on slips.
2 The teams sort the slips into order from high to low.
3 Teams walk around and discuss or argue with others.
4 Elicit a general pattern.

Examples: Ranking of

• university departments for academic prestige;
• professions for status;
• teaching methods for how much is learnt;
• indicators for how easy they are to measure;
• politicians for honesty.

Tips and options

• Sorting is best done standing around tables or on the ground.
• Be prepared for dissent. It may lead to better understanding.
• Where there is dissent encourage debate.

17 Video learning

A participant, facilitator or other person takes short videos of key learning, for example:

• short interviews with participants, asking them what they have learnt;
• key sequences, for example, of feedback and reflection sessions;
• highlights of the experience;
• illustrations of facilitators' and participants' behaviour.

These are edited and shown.

VIDEO LEARNING

Tips and options

- Avoid major disruption to the sequence of events.
- Do not show too much.
- Short key learning from participants both reinforce what has been learnt and provide a record.
- Give participants a video cassette of what their peers have said to take home.

18 Collegial learning through helping

An all-win solution when participants have different levels of comprehension or knowledge. Those with more help those with less.

This method appears widely applicable. It works well when the language of a workshop is not the lingua franca of the group, and some understand better and others less well. It turns the problem into an opportunity for learning, discussion and collegial support in groups. Those who understand better have to concentrate on what is said. They reinforce their learning and memory by telling their colleagues, who also learn by hearing the content twice, once less well understood in plenary, and once from their colleagues, usually in their mother tongue.

- Ask participants to stand and cluster into those who know more or understand better and those who know less or understand less well.
- Depending on relative sizes of cluster, ask them to form ones, twos or threes, etc, and team up in mixed groups [see **11**:12].
- Present topics briefly without translation. Then give time for those who understand better to put the others more in the picture. Discussion usually takes place as well.
- Continue

19 Review, reflect and share

For reinforcing and extending learning

Open-ended evaluations of workshops tend to single out such periods of reflection as important for learning. But good participatory processes often overrun and squeeze out time at the end. Yet the payoffs from reflection are high precisely when participation has been good and a lot has been experienced but not recalled, reviewed or written down.

So, make space to reflect *immediately after an experience*. This applies with various of the 21s, and especially with experiential practicals, methods and processes. After a person or group has had an experience, invite reflection on, for example, some or all of:

* What happened?
* What did you experience?
* What did you learn?
* What difference will it make to you?

Tips and options

* Set time aside for reflection, say two–five minutes at the end of a session, or seven–ten at the end of a day.
* Mention that time has been set aside, put it on the programme and stick to it (easier said than done).
* Start with individual reflection in complete silence.
* Invite people individually to note what they have learnt or gained.
* Do it yourself.
* Conclude with quiet discussion with neighbours and/or with feedback to plenary (perhaps the next session or the next morning).
* Reflection can also be in groups instead of individually.

20 So what? A final analysis

For consolidating and developing what has been covered and learnt. In a workshop or course, reserve a last period or session for group discussion and analysis of what has been covered, followed by presentations in plenary.

This is for further digestion of material, not regurgitation. Ideally, it is linked with follow-up action. Two examples from workshops are:

What are you going to do?

* contact others;
* read new material;
* network;
* introduce others to new ideas;
* convene meetings;
* write;
* advocate;

and so on?

What are the implications for more general action and policy?

The learning and follow-up can be consolidated through listing on flip charts, and then through spoken presentation to plenary.

21 Improvise, invent and share

21 Tips on How to Avoid Lecturing

Is your lecture really necessary?

Is the answer to this question more often 'No' than most talking teachers realize?

For some of us, lecturing can become a masochistic addiction. We are nervous. We prepare. We gear ourselves up. There is a sequence and rhythm to our internal shots of adrenalin. At the peak, we deliver. Crisis, catharsis and consummation follow. And then coffee and collapse.

Complain though we do, many of us like this ritual. It strokes the ego. We stand up in front of all those children, students, probationers, newcomers or participants. We are important and knowledgeable. After all, *We* know. And we know that *they (lower case)* don't know. To impart our knowledge is a pleasurable duty. We fill the empty vessels. And if the vessels are already full, they hide the spillage from our sight. So we lecture. We teach.

But teaching and learning are not the same thing.

Source: based on an original idea by Bud Blake.

To be sure, there is a place for lecturing. A good lecture is well structured, clearly delivered, entertaining, informative and stimulating. At its best it is an art form. But lecturing and learning are not one-for-one the same thing. Those who listen are usually passive. After 15 minutes or so, most minds wander (I generalize from a sample of one with which I am familiar). In contrast, much good learning is interactive, through analysis, discussion and reflection.

These tips are short and sharp. They supplement tips elsewhere. Their point is to ram home that alternatives exist and point to ideas of what can be done. If this is new to you, try just this: *break up your lecture with buzzes.*

If you are teaching a technical subject and don't see how to avoid lecturing, see 21 Ways to Help Each Other Learn [**16**].

There are many things you can do. Here are some. As with the other 21s, enjoy.

1 Book a big flat room

The tiers of seats in the traditional lecture theatre are a trap: the physical set up programmes you like a puppet. You pontificate. Go instead for a big flat room with the freedom of plenty of space and scope to decentre authority.

2 Make even more space

Put tables around the walls and chairs in the middle. Leave space for walking around.

3 Arrange informal seating

Have chairs in almost any pattern except formal schoolroom lines. One or more U shapes, muddled up, can be good, or a circle of chairs, or concentric circles of chairs [see **12**].

4 Use wall charts

Minimize overhead transparencies and maximize wall charts. These stay there, can be referred back to by anyone, and can be copied out without rushing.

5 When you have to talk, keep it to ten minutes

Seems crazy. Most people can listen and take in for longer. But set ten as a target. Announce this as a personal rule. Most of us, giving ourselves ten, take 15. Maybe if you say ten you will keep down to 15. You could do worse. Say what will happen after the ten (15) minutes, and how that fits and follows on.

6 Don't tell people what they can discover for themselves
[See **14**; **15**; and **16**].

7 Use buzzes

Break into small discussion groups. Groups of three are good. If you say groups of three some will form fours, even fives. So go for three. The smaller the group, the more those who are shy will feel able to talk.

8 Warn when a buzz is coming

The warning encourages active and critical listening and reflection during the preceding activity.

9 Walk around, listen and help during buzzes

But beware of sabotaging discussions. And don't worry if you need the time to regroup and prepare for the next activity. This is not exactly new for primary school teachers!

10 Limit or postpone feedback from buzzes

Sounds wrong but can make sense, especially with large numbers. Feedback often means the same old people talking and others keeping quiet. You can instead…

11 Collect questions to be discussed later

Questions and issues can be listed. Have a flip chart or sticky sheet on which they can be written or stuck up [see **13**:19].

12 Invite participants to answer their own questions first

If they can. This takes the heat off you, encourages those able to respond, and can reveal who has special knowledge.

13 Find and use experience and knowledge in the group

This is so easy to overlook. People with relevant knowledge and experience are usually better at helping their peers to learn than an external authority figure.

FIND KNOWLEDGE IN THE GROUP

14 Facilitate lateral learning

Help participants to help one another. For example, ask who understands or knows something, and who does not, and then pair or group those who do with those who do not.

15 Be optimally unprepared

Do not plan every minute. Have a core agenda plus a repertoire of things to do, so that you can respond creatively to issues that arise [see **13**:4].

16 Avoid a fixed time to end

A session that goes well may not need to end 'on time'. Negotiate and agree a right time to finish. Minimize timetables which run with sessions back to back. But be sensitive to others' deadlines like collecting a child from a nursery or catching a train.

17 Decentre and move around

Reduce the dominance and authority of one part of the room. Do not stay in the same place all the time. Move around and sit or stand in different places. This breaks monotony and reduces your dominance. Sitting away from the head of the room (with its blackboard, screen and so on) can encourage conversations between participants, not just between them and you [see also **12** for seating options].

18 Help others move

It helps to walk and stand, especially in the late morning and the 'graveyard session' of early afternoon. Show and tell with wall charts is a good way to do this. ('Now let's get up and go and look at the chart on the wall over there.')

19 Give yourself breathers

Use buzzes and group and individual learning activities to give yourself time to regroup and prepare to make the next part participatory.

20 Odd-rows-rise-and-reverse

When trapped by an amphitheatre-like lecture hall [see **12**:1], ask the odd rows to stand up, turn around and buzz with those behind them, who stay seated. Usually heads are roughly level. The first time you do this expect a short stunned silence, and then an electric explosion of talking.

21 Invent, experiment, improvise and share

Surely you can improve on these few tips. And please tell the rest of us.

Part 6
Behaviour and Awareness

21 Activities for Attitude and Behaviour Awareness and Change

Personal behaviour, attitudes and commitment are central to participation and to institutional and professional change. Fittingly, Attitude and Behaviour Change has been described as the ABC of PRA [see **21**:7]. So this is one of the more important of the 21s. Perhaps too it is also the one merits the most further work.

These exercises are meant to combine effectiveness, ease of facilitation and acceptability to participants. Effectiveness refers to providing experiences which may help to enhance self-awareness and lead to personal change. To facilitate them does not, I think, require therapeutic training of the sort demanded by deeper psychological approaches. I have also selected activities acceptable across a broad spectrum from senior government officers and political leaders to villagers and slum dwellers.

For complementary exercises see **19**, which concerns deterring dominators and helping shy people to speak, and the section on multiple realities in **14**:1–6, which concerns others' realities and how we see one another.

These 21 are not a panacea. They are not the stuff of sudden conversions, of scales falling from the eyes. Do not expect dramatic flips from, say, hardened dominator and saboteur to sensitive listener and facilitator. But they may sow some seeds which germinate and flower over time.

Some suggestions may help:

- *Atmosphere.* Set a friendly, informal and non-threatening atmosphere for a workshop, course or training from the very first. Ideally this will start before-hand with selection so that those who come want to come, followed where feasible by a welcoming note and information, and sometimes a task, sent in advance [see **2**:15]. Then the way the experience is introduced is important [see **5**].
- *Joking words.* Establish words as part of a joking culture of the group. Saboteur and Dominator are two good ones.
- *Share your mistakes.* Set an example yourself with self-critical sharing of mistakes. Something always goes wrong, often because of some omission or error one has made. If you can, in a non-defensive way, mention this, regret it and say 'That was a mistake. Sorry. But GOOD, because it is an opportunity to learn'. This will make it easier for others to do the same

- *Relax and relax others.* Introduce activities in a friendly non-dominating way, and encourage participants.
- *Criticize as little as possible.* Enjoy, and help others to find in the experiences both food for reflection and fun. Appreciate and help those who are threatened and find all this difficult.
- *Energizers.* Use energizers and games throughout. They help in loosening up so that more is gained from ABC activities [see **6**].
- *Seating.* Remember that relationships are influenced by arrangements of seating [see **12**].
- *Democracy of the ground.* As and when you can, get down on to the ground. It is an equalizer and changes relationships. Consider whether activities can be done on the ground, and use it where it fits and makes sense [see **12**:18; **14**:16; and **19**:17].

Much of what follows can be benignly infectious fun.

Contents

1	Uppers and lowers	12	Acting another
2	Saboteur	13	In a group I mainly…
3	Dominator	14	Positive incident
4	Self-assessment	15	Who says what, behaving how?
5	Sculpting statues	16	Non-verbal circles
6	What do you see?	17	Mapping interactions
7	Chairs	18	Colleague card sort
8	Lowers as teachers (LAST)	19	Silence
9	Interested and bored	20	Video playback
10	Listening to understand	21	Invent, experiment and share your own exercises
11	Dos and don'ts		

1 Uppers and lowers

A good starter to get into the topic with awareness and analysis of dominant–subordinate, upper–lower, relationships. The core with many variants is:

Listing of upper–lower relationships

Such as parent–child, senior–junior, teacher–student, boss–secretary (there are an extraordinary number). [See **15**:5].

Reflection and discussion

Options include

Individual, group and/or plenary reflection and discussion of:

- upper and lower behaviours;
- how upper–lower relationships reinforce each other in chains like magnets;
- how they distort communication (how all power deceives);
- how uppers are disabled from learning.

Quiet personal reflection, listing and sharing in a small group of:

- relationships in which I am a lower;
- how uppers behave and treat me and how I feel;
- relationships in which I am an upper;
- how as an upper I behave and treat lowers (and they are likely to feel).

and then

- Are there ways I would like to change my upper behaviour?
- Are there ways I would like to change my lower behaviour?

Uppers and lowers leads well into *Dominator* (3 below) and discussions of dominant realities.

2 Saboteur

An enjoyable icebreaker and energizer to heighten awareness of our sabotaging behaviour.

Allow 15–60 minutes, depending on the depth of
the reflection and discussion. Divide into threes. Two
are speakers and one the saboteur. The speakers talk
about a subject both are interested in. The saboteur
interrupts, disrupts or distracts in any non-violent
manner, variously verbal or non-verbal, subtle or unsubtle.

SABOTEUR

Tips and options

- Allow two–five minutes for each turn.
- Have a grace period. Tell saboteurs to listen and wait a bit before starting, or give a signal after 30 seconds or so for them to start.
- Give each person a go with each role (best, given time, but just one round is enough for reflection and learning).
- You, and anyone left out, go round as roving saboteurs, interrupting by asking groups how they are getting on. (This usually stops the activity, with all looking at this new saboteur.)
- Do not announce that it is saboteur. Ask groups of three to decide that two will talk and one listen or observe. Brief the listener/observers separately. This adds realism as the talkers do not know what to expect.

- Complete 'I am a saboteur when ...' Invite quiet reflection and noting, and then sharing in small groups.
- Encourage 'saboteur' to become part of the joking culture of the group. Stick up the word 'Saboteur' in several places as a reminder.
- Use it as a joke against yourself when you interrupt others, to show awareness of your own behaviour. Point out that asking threes how they were doing was a form of sabotage.

Reflection and discussion

Merge threes to make groups of six to discuss the experience, followed by plenary sharing. This may be enough, but additional options are:

Questions that can be asked in plenary include:

- What is it like to be a saboteur or to be sabotaged?
- Do you find it easy or difficult to disrupt others' conversations?
- What are the different types of saboteur?
- What different forms does sabotage take?
- How can you deal with a saboteur?
- How can groups deal with saboteur individuals, etc?

A fun short sequence in plenary is to ask for hands to be raised for:

- Who has had the experience of being in the middle of a sentence when a senior person (or upper) starts talking and you have to shut up? (usually all hands go up).
- What does it feel like? (usually awful, humiliating, I feel angry ...).
- Have you ever done it to others? (wryly, usually yes).

Sources: various including *Participatory Learning and Action: A Trainer's Guide* [see **21**:1, pp160–161]

3 Dominator

A lively activity to heighten awareness of verbal and non-verbal dominant and submissive behaviour and of the effects of physical position on relationships.

This follows well after *Uppers and lowers and Saboteur*. Allow some 25 to 50 minutes:

- five–ten minutes for briefing and preparation;
- up to ten minutes for the role play;
- 15–30 minutes for reflection and discussion.

Process

1   Participants sit in groups of three, each on a chair. They choose one person (a good talker!) to be dominator (the 'upper'), one to be dominated (the 'lower'), and one to be an observer.

2   While the upper and the lower decide the role and context in which the dominator will assert her/himself, call the observers aside and brief them about what will happen, and alert them to observe process, verbal and non-verbal behaviour, changing relationships, etc.
3   With all three in each group sitting on chairs, and the upper and the lower facing each other, ask the uppers to start dominating.
4   After two–three minutes, tell the lower to sit on the floor.
5   After a further two–three minutes, tell the upper and lower to change positions, with the upper on the floor and the lower on a chair. (Tell the dominating upper to keep going!)
6   After two–three more minutes, participants sit in groups of six and discuss and reflect on the experience.
7   Invite each group to share one or two insights or reflections with the plenary.

Tips and options

*   If done without chairs, all sit on the floor for the first round. For the second, the upper stands. Finally, the lower stands while the upper sits.
*   Do not rush the final discussions (stages 6 and 7 above). Sometimes a lot comes out, and participants learn by talking things through.
*   'I am a dominator when…' Invite quiet reflection and noting, and then sharing in small groups.
*   Encourage 'dominator' to become part of the joking culture of the group. Stick up the word 'Dominator' in several places as a reminder. In one training experience, a talkative and dominant participant said:

    'I am not only a dominator. I am a saboteur.'

4 Self-assessment

A good activity for critical self-awareness. Straightforward to facilitate.

Process

Allow 5–60 minutes, depending on number of characteristics and depth of discussion.

1   Choose, or invite participants to choose, one or more personal characteristics for self-assessment. Examples are tendency to interrupt others, ability to accept criticism, self-assertiveness, 'how participatory are you?' and 'how easy you find it to hand over the stick'? Or brainstorm a list of polar personal characteristics, for example, reactive–proactive, centralizing–delegating, cautious–risk taking, organized–disorganized, sceptical–naive, diffident–outspoken and so on.
2   Participants represent their self-assessment by where they stand along a line between extremes. *With a larger group*, stick up or mark on the floor numbers from 0 to 10, and ask participants to stand by their score. *With a smaller group*, they can stand between two poles without using numbers.
3   All discuss with neighbours why they have put themselves where they are.

4   *Option.* All move to where they were say five years earlier and discuss.
5   All move to where they would like to be in, say, two years' time, and discuss what they have to do to get there.

Tips and options

- Works best when participants have loosened up and are relaxed with one another. Better following than preceding *Saboteur* and *Dominator*. A good way to conclude a session or day on ABC, leading into quiet reflection.
- Take part yourself.
- After discussion, participants can be asked if they wish to reposition themselves.
- When participants know one another well, light-hearted disagreements with others' self-assessments can help.
- Reflect and discuss further, in plenary or groups.
- Collect and write up striking remarks made by participants.

Sources: Kausar Khan, *Gender Training Manual* (Khan, 1996), which uses this (page 15) for self-assertiveness training, Jethro Pettit and Patta Scott-Villiers.

5 Sculpting statues

For awareness of messages we send with our body positions and language. Allow 5–20 minutes.

Form groups of four. Two are sculptors and two are clay. The sculptors arrange the clay persons to represent a relationship, or attitudes and behaviours. Examples are generous and grateful, dominant and submissive, angry and pacifying... The sculptures hold their positions. The sculptors walk around and see what others have done.
     Repeat, reversing sculptor–clay roles.

Tips and options

- Precede this with an energizer.
- Be sensitive to culture, especially aspects of gender if touching between the sexes is inappropriate.
- After the first sculpture, invite either sculptors or the sculpted to change the relationship.
- The many variants include creating group scenarios, discussed then in plenary.
- Reflect and discuss the significance of body positions and language.

6 What do you see?

For analysis and reflection on contexts, behaviours, body language and forms of interaction. Allow 5–30 minutes.

Find or prepare visuals or sets of visuals which show interactions and relationships. These can be sets of photographs (from newspapers and magazines, or from your own or others' collections), drawings or cartoons, or wall charts with photographs, or a number of slides. These can illustrate degrees of formality–informality, hostility–friendliness, exclusion–inclusion of women and poor people etc.

Present the visuals and invite observation, analysis and discussion. These take different forms according to the materials. For example:

With visuals on walls, get up, stand and discuss.

With sets of photographs, drawings or cartoons, form groups. Each group receives an identical set and compares and analyses the examples it presents. Plenary sharing can follow.

With videos options include showing without a soundtrack, replaying, and stopping and studying a still frame.

Tips and options

- Protect photos or drawings with plastic or put them in transparent sleeves if you want them to last.
- Avoid showing too many slides.
- Photographs or pictures can be ranked for a criterion such as degree of informality, participation, or inclusion of women and poor people, etc, or matrix scored [see **15**:7–8] for several criteria. Compare and discuss the rankings by different groups.
- With a large group, a good sequence is analysis of a set of photographs followed by discussion of projected slides of the same pictures.

Source: Carolyn Jones

7 Chairs

A versatile exercise to explore how physical arrangements and positions reflect and influence relationships [see **12**]. Many variants can be invented or will happen. Allow 10–30 minutes.

ABC CHAIRS

You need chairs (say four–ten for a single group). A table and other props like a glass of water, clipboard or pad can also help. There are many options and combinations:

- Ask participants to arrange the chairs to reflect different relationships. Compare and discuss.
- Arrange the table and chairs to express authority and dominance. Ask participants to analyse and then make a series of changes to the arrangements. Compare and discuss.
- Ask participants to arrange two sets of chairs, one to reflect teaching, and one facilitation. Compare and discuss.

- Participants sit in the chairs and are modelled or model themselves as statues for non-verbal ways of showing relationships.
- Participants sit in the chairs and act out roles (sometimes this just happens without prompting).
- Participants improvise and invent their own patterns of seating.

Variants

- Small paper or cardboard cut-outs represent chairs, tables of different sorts, a screen, a blackboard, etc, and are arranged by participants in different patterns, which are then compared and discussed.
- Participants make sketchmaps of their offices, leaving space for comments. The sketches are shuffled up and then circulated. Participants write comments and suggestions on the sketches. At the end, each retrieves her or his sketch, and reflects on the comments.
- Photocopies of selected seating arrangements [from **12**, or redrawn] are compared and matrix scored in groups.

Tip

- Discussion may flow or be led in several directions such as how changing seating and position changes interactions and relationships, and spatial aspects of empowerment (for participants) and self-disempowerment (by a facilitator).

8 Lowers as teachers (LAST)

An activity which reverses relationships and shows uppers they have much to learn from lowers. Negotiate with lowers to teach uppers a task or activity. Uppers then learn and perform the task under instruction. Reflect on the experience.

Applications

There are many opportunities in everyday life – for parents to be taught by children, bosses by secretaries, priests by lay people, doctors by patients, facilitators by participants... In PRA field learning, villagers or slum dwellers teach those who are participating in the experience [see **14**:10].

Tip

Record on video and play it back.

9 Interested and bored

For awareness of how our behaviour affects one another. The frustration and embarrassment generated is usually released at the end in laughter and learning. Allow 15–20 minutes if roles are reversed, and a total of 30–40 minutes with discussions and plenary.

All sit in pairs. One is to talk, the other listen. The talker is to pick a subject she or he cares about and is interested in.

Brief the listeners where the talkers cannot hear. Tell them to listen intently at first, showing much interest, and then gradually to become more and more bored. Give an indication how much time they have.

Tips and options

- The listener listens intently for a prearranged duration, or until you give a sign (a cough, or clap, or walking close), and then gradually acts more and more bored.
- Tell everyone what will happen. This is less powerful but less manipulative.
- Be sensitive if the medium is a language in which some are not very fluent.
- Be alert and ready to intervene if any talker who is not being listened to shows distress.
- After one round, reverse the roles.
- Ask pairs to form groups of four or six and discuss how it felt.
- Invite reflections in plenary.

10 Listening to understand

For learning how to listen to understand another person's realities.

Process

Allow anything from 15–60 minutes.

1 Explain how badly we often listen. The purpose is to practise listening in order to understand another person's reality, what they think, their values, enthusiasms, convictions and the like.
2 Make two rules for the exercise:

Do: Affirm what the other is saying. Show that you understand. When in doubt repeat back what you think she or he has said. Say what you think she or he must be feeling.

Don't: Criticize or put forward your own views or ideas.

3 Divide into pairs or threes. Ask one person to talk to another about something she or he cares about, while the other listens to understand. If you have threes, one observes and feeds back at the end. Say five minutes for this.
4 Ask the listener to repeat back what she or he has heard, the first speaker to give feedback on whether they have really been understood, and the observer, if there is one, to comment.
5 Repeat changing the roles until all have talked and listened.

Tips and options

- This fits quite well after *Interested and bored*.
- A short demonstration by you or someone else helps to show what is entailed. (If you do it yourself and mess up, as I have done, use this as an example of embracing error and learning from it. That will put others at ease and make it easier for them also to admit and learn from mistakes.)
- Phrases like 'if I understand you, what you are saying is ...' 'so what you are feeling is ...' 'You mean ...' can be used, but let everyone find their own words and way of showing they have heard and understood.

11 Dos and don'ts

Straightforward, participatory, versatile and strong. For analysis and awareness of possible good and bad facilitation and behaviours. Allow 10–30 minutes.

Brainstorm and list dos and don'ts for behaviours, for example:

- listening;
- facilitating;
- dealing with big talkers, dominators or saboteurs;
- helping people who feel shy or threatened;
- becoming more aware of one's behaviour;
- achieving good teamwork.

Share, discuss and consolidate.

Options for feedback

[See **15**:13–17.]

12 Acting another

For seeing and understanding how we and others behave. Allow 30–60 minutes.

Form pairs. In each pair, one person is A, the other B. B prepares to act out how A would behave in a selected situation. Allow perhaps ten minutes for each pair to choose a situation and to discuss how A would behave in it.

B then acts out the situation, with continual guidance from A who has the benefit of seeing his/her own behaviour from the outside. Repeat with A acting out B's behaviour. Form groups of four to share and discuss the experience.

ACTING ANOTHER

There are many possible situations, for example:

- delivering a reprimand;
- conducting a staff appraisal;
- presenting a complaint to someone senior;
- interviewing a candidate;
- facilitating a PRA activity;
- entering a community;
- chairing a monthly staff meeting;
- addressing a community meeting.

Apologies to unidentified source. This is from your page 62.

13 In a group I mainly ...

For reflecting on one's own behaviour and how we are seen by others. The basic sequence is: (1) Identify personal behaviours or roles; (2) Join others who are similar; (3) Discuss; (4) Share. There are options at each stage and scope for more.

1 *Either* make a list yourself of personal behaviours or roles, or facilitate a brain-storm to complete the sentence 'In a group I mainly ...' or 'In a group I am a ...' Keep the list fairly short (say four–six). Examples of behaviours are listen, think, argue, lead, facilitate, and of roles, listener, thinker, debater, leader, facilitator.
2 *Either* post up the words in different parts of the room and all move quickly to which represents them best or all reflect individually and write rankings for themselves for the behaviours or roles and then find others who are similar and form groups.
3 Groups discuss their role or behaviour and:
    - What about it is helpful?
    - What about it is unhelpful?
    - How do others see you?
    - Do you want to make any changes?
    - Any other reflections?
4 The groups stay together and share their insights with the rest (often with laughter). Others can question their insights.

Tips and options

- Encourage people to move fast at stage 2. If any do not choose they can form their own group.
- When insights are being questioned keep it light-hearted.
- Discussion can recognize the value of all the behaviours and roles.
- After 4, add 5: Form groups for your lowest ranked role or behaviour. Discuss. Share.

Source: adapted from *Training for Transformation: A Handbook for Community Workers* [see **21**:9, Vol 2, pp65–66].

14 Positive incident

For sharing and exploring behaviour which overcomes difficulties. Allow 20–40 minutes.

Explain that the purpose is to learn from one another's experience. Sometimes we overcome a difficulty we have with a colleague or peer, or someone with whom we have to work. Give a personal example. Mention that overcoming the difficulty is often not easy and may involve swallowing one's pride and making a big effort.

Ask everyone to think of a personal example. Take time for this. Then invite sharing in pairs or small groups of three or four.

Options

- Plenary sharing at the end.
- Brainstorm a list of actions that were taken, share these and discuss.

Source: Development Support Centre Workshop, Ahmedabad 1998.

15 Who says what, behaving how?

For identifying and exploring typical critical views, and the behaviour that goes with them. Allow 20–40 minutes.

Invite groups to brainstorm and list cynical and critical remarks they have heard. These can be about participation, development, transparency, NGOs, senior staff, junior staff, women, minorities… Choose only one of these, or only one at a time.

The remarks are listed in the centre of a chart, on the left who made or makes the remark, and on the right what behaviour goes with it. Discuss.

Source: Development Support Centre Workshop, Ahmedabad 1998.

16 Non-verbal circles

A lively way to see how non-verbal behaviour expresses attitudes such as dominance, submissiveness and friendliness.

Process

Allow 15–20 minutes.

1 Ask groups of five to ten people to stand in circles, facing inwards.
2 Each group shows and performs as many non-verbal actions as they can that demonstrate, say, dominating behaviour. Anyone identifies and does an action, and then all in the group repeat it.
3 Continue until one or two groups are running out of ideas.
4 Each group chooses its best non-verbal action, and then sits down.
5 Groups stand up in turn and show the others their best one.
6 Repeat for other characteristics like submissiveness and 'being nice to people'.

Tips and options

- This is best preceded by an energizing group-former, for example, *Jungle* [see **11**:4].
- A round-up discussion can elicit observations about types of postures and gestures.
- The importance of eyes in showing what a person is thinking and feeling is missed in this exercise. Discuss this. Demonstrate by putting on dark glasses and asking people what you are thinking. So why do film stars wear them?

17 Mapping interactions

A striking exercise with immediate impact, learning about and often changing awareness and behaviour [see **19**:14].

One or more volunteers observe and map. Discuss with the observer(s) what to observe and how to record. Examples of *what* are:

- Who speaks, how many times, and for how long.
- Who does not speak.
- Who interrupts.
- Who is and who is not recognized by the chair.
- Who listens and does not listen to whom.
- Who looks at whom while talking.
- Side conversations, between whom, and why.
- Body language (arms crossed, looking at the clock, etc).

Examples of *how* are:

- List speakers and enter number of seconds for each time they speak. Circle when stopped by an interruption.
- Mark interrupters and numbers of interruptions.
- Draw a circle round the speaker each time she or he speaks.
- Use arrows to indicate who is talking to whom.
- Use dotted circles and dotted arrows for side conversations.

But improvise and develop your own. Analysis of the interactions can be by:

- female and male;
- age;
- seniority;
- language fluency;
- ethnic group;

as appropriate and shared back with the whole group. Note that observers also learn a lot from this.

Tips

- Allow plenty of time for feedback and discussion. It can be quite intense.
- Observing is itself an education. It also distracts from the substance of a discussion. You may therefore want to rotate the role of monitor.
- Reflect on and review changes over the duration of a course or workshop.

Source: Andrea Cornwall for ideas about mini-ethnographies of meetings, and Koy Thompson and others, ActionAid workshop, Dhaka, February 2001.

18 Colleague card sort

An intense and concentrated experience, often with laughter and joking, showing how we see others' behaviour and they see ours.

This requires that the group know one another, usually having been together for several days or weeks. A workshop after some days, or a course or regular seminar, are suitable if numbers are not large. Choose a characteristic for sorting and ranking. Examples are ability to listen, teamwork and gender sensitivity (for which I have never forgotten failing to be ranked as good). [See **19**:11].

Participants form teams of three–five. Each team makes a set of name cards with one card for each participant in the whole group. So each team has the same full set of names. Give them, or ask them to choose, a characteristic for sorting or ranking. They then sort or rank the cards on the ground or floor, or less good, on tables.

Display, compare and discuss.

Tips and options

- Do this after an energizer when all are animated.
- Do not include too sensitive a characteristic too early in a group getting to know one another.
- Form groups and let them decide the characteristic(s).
- Invite participatory analysis to correlate characteristics (obvious, but I have no experience of this).

19 Silence

One of those short, simple, dramatic things that people remember. This is to show the difficulty and empowering effects of keeping silent. You need a little courage and determination, and less than five minutes.

SILENCE

Introduce the subject of talking and silence. Describe how in a classroom or lecture situation the teacher or lecturer feels the need to keep talking, to fill time with words, but how, to empower others, it is sometimes necessary to sit down and shut up. Then sit on the ground and say nothing for one minute. (Time it.) Often participants are embarrassed. Some may start talking to each other at the back. Or they may encourage you to stand up again. The speech and the initiative are passed to them.

20 Video playback

As powerful as any other exercise. To increase awareness of how we behave and how we appear to others. You need a video camera, a well-briefed camera operator (or do it yourself), and facilities for playback.

Take a video of participants (and why not also yourself) interacting, for example, in group discussions, or being taught by villagers, or during an interview.

Preview this, especially if it is likely to embarrass anyone. Play it back to the group.

Tips and options

* Stop at key points and analyse single frames.
* Fast forward over parts which might embarrass too much.
* Show to members of any community involved.
* Invite participants to use the camera themselves subsequently.
* Encourage participants to play back to themselves later.
* Re-enact with different behaviour, and playback again.

21 Invent, experiment and share your own exercises

21 Tips for Dealing with Dominators and Helping the Silent Speak (if they *want* to, that is)

I have not yet met a trainer, teacher or course convenor who has not faced a problem with dominators. These are typically people who talk a lot. Less widely recognized is the problem of those who are intimidated, threatened, quiet, shy and silent.

On the positive side, dominators and big talkers often have good things to say. Often they are leaders. For their part, those who are withdrawn and quiet may have silence as a strategy for self-protection. They may wish to exercise an inalienable human right not to speak. If so, should we be sensitive and not force things? One option is to give them a copy of 21 tips for surviving participatory workshops [see **20**], which you are not meant to know about, the better to defend themselves.

On the negative side, dominant big talkers often waste time, take things off at a tangent, annoy and inhibit other participants, and make you mad. They also disable themselves by losing opportunities to learn from others. For their part, those who are silent or speak little are not sharing their experience, and are not learning in the way we learn through talking. They often have more to contribute than either they or we realize. Giving silent people space and encouragement to speak may matter more than shutting up those who talk too much. But each process can help the other.

So, while respecting individual diversity, we can look for humane ways to optimize, helping some to speak less and others to speak more. The goal could be called interactive equity. The aim is not equal air time but fair shares: to liberate the loquacious from their disability, not gag them; to empower the reticent, not expose them; to help quiet people gain confidence in speaking out if they want to. These are reversals of upper–lower dominance and submission, helping uppers to restrain themselves and lowers to express themselves.

This could be dreadfully serious, painful and confrontational. We all have our personal styles in how we handle this. Mine is to go for non-threatening, light-hearted self-awareness. This looks rather superficial but my hunch is that it works fairly well. But others have deeper, more reflective approaches, as in *Training for Transformation* (Hope and Timmel, 1984 [see **21**:9]). These can be expected to have more profound and lasting effects. As ever, there is a lot to be said for diversity of approaches and mutual learning.

There is some general advice:

- Make it safe for people to see and say things about themselves.
- Let learning come from experience and reflection, not lecturing.
- Let laughter and fun play a part.
- When in doubt, be nice to people. Thus:

> To deal with the dread dominator
> make love. Do not hate him or hate her
> The key is – Defer
> Say to him or to her
> Thanks a lot. We'll make time for you later

> To deal with the dire saboteur
> Playfully sabotage him or her
> With generous tact
> Find a means to distract
> With sweet nothings, red herrings, or beer

Contents

1 In the open, from the start

Raise the issue right at the start. Say there is a common problem. Some talk a lot. Others stay silent. Whether naturally loquacious or naturally reticent, no one should feel threatened. We learn both by listening and by talking. We all need to talk. We all need to listen. We need to strive towards equity in talking time and listening time, and will give one another honest feedback. We need to be especially sensitive to different levels of fluency in the language of the workshop or course, frequently English but also French, Hindi, Mandarin, Portuguese, Russian, Spanish and others. Those for whom the language is their native tongue often have a sharp advantage over those for whom it is second or third, who may have difficulty understanding and contributing. One way to make these issues clear at the outset is through 'Buses' [see **5**:10] and subsequent discussion.

2 Give turns

This is a most common and effective device. Say politely 'You have already spoken. Let us hear from someone else', or 'Who has not yet had a chance?'.

This requires a deliberate effort. Certain people, especially when disabled by being older, male, senior, garrulous, self-important, used to being treated with deference, and equipped with a deep and loud voice, tend to get recognized and allowed to speak. You have to help everyone, themselves included, by offsetting this.

3 Hold the conch

Choose, or better let the group choose, an object – a ball, a book, a pen, or whatever (for Native Americans this has been the 'talking stone'; in William Golding's book *Lord of the Flies* it was a conch shell) – which gives authority to speak. Only the person who holds it may talk. Others must wait. When finished, the speaker hands it on to someone else.

This promotes the idea of taking turns and listening, regulates itself, draws attention to who talks and who does not, reduces interruptions, and can give time and confidence to some who otherwise might have kept quiet.

Tip

Use sparingly. Overused it can inhibit the free flow of ideas, and even allow some to dominate.

4 Give a responsible role

Recognize those who tend to dominate and give them responsible roles. To chair the meeting can work but carries risks. Safer are dealing with problems like logistics, relations with a community, or a visiting saboteur. One of the best is to *make big talkers observers and recorders*. Brief them to sit outside a group, keep quiet, observe and record what goes on – behaviour, interactions, who talks most and least and then to give feedback and reflections at the end (as in Talkers map – see 14 below).

For anyone who tends to be left out or marginalized, a responsible but non-threatening role can enhance their confidence and self-esteem and the respect which others show them.

5 Take out

Invite the talker out of the group. Exploit his or her special knowledge. Empower him or her to have his or her knowledge and views recorded.

Sometimes this is an act of desperation, with the sacrifice of a facilitator to do the job. Usually, though, there is a good deal to be gained. The big talker often knows much that is of value.

When a team member takes a person out, it makes for appreciation and a good spirit in the team.

6 Ration: matchsticks and the candy game

Remarks can be rationed in several ways so that frequent talkers find they have to shut up. Two of these are:

Matchsticks. For group discussions each counts out five (or some other number) matchsticks (or seeds, stones, etc). Each time a person speaks, they put one of their matchsticks (or seeds, stones, etc) into the centre. When they have none left, they cannot say any more.

Follow with reflection on how it felt. Encourage 'matchsticks' as a joking part of the group culture, said whenever anyone talks too much.

CANDY GAME

The candy game. Obtain largish hard sweets. Whoever makes a comment is rewarded with a sweet to be popped in the mouth. Only sucking is then allowed. Anyone who participates too much soon finds further speech problematical.

One talkative head of an organization stayed dominant by munching the sweets, and became known as 'our teeth-using friend'.

Sources: matchsticks, lost in the mists of time; the candy game, Alex Hay.

7 Send on

After a buzz or small group session, ask each group to identify who spoke most, and then send that person on to a new group. Warn the new group (joking) that they are getting another big talker.

8 Regroup

After a buzz or group discussion, ask each group to rank its members by how much they have talked. Form new groups of high talkers together, medium talkers together, and low talkers together – as many new groups as make sense.

Options

- The initial groups can be invited to stand in parallel lines, with those who have talked most at the head, and those who have talked least at the tail. This heightens awareness, and grouping is then easy.

- In the new groups, the buzz or group discussion can continue on the same topic. Participants share what was discussed in their earlier group.

9 Warn visitors

This applies when others come to conduct sessions. It is astonishingly neglected. I do not remember ever having been warned in advance about dominant talkers in a group. By the time a visitor has learnt who talks too much, the session is over. The pattern then repeats with the next visitor, and the dominator has his (more rarely her) way session after session, with escalating irritation to others in the group. A discrete warning in advance is all that is needed. Or a discrete enquiry by the visitor.

10 Senior silence

Ask all senior (or otherwise upper or loquacious) people not to speak for a period (ten minutes, an hour, a session, a morning or afternoon, even a day). In the early stages, repeated reminders may be needed. Invite reflection later, both by the senior people, and by others.

11 Talkativeness ranking

Ask groups to write their colleagues' names on slips of paper. When they are ready, ask them to rank the slips on the ground according to high and low talkativeness in sessions. Then encourage comparison between groups.

SENIOR SILENCE

This works well with a course that has been together for some time. It can also be used in small groups referring to a discussion just completed. It can be very animated and much fun.

Tip

Encourage reflection and discussion. It may be best to stress that it is not necessarily bad to be at one of the extremes, especially so that those ranked as talking least do not feel bad.

12 Write up to remind

Write up words after exercises and display these in prominent places. Examples are 'Dominator', 'Saboteur', and 'Matchsticks'. Encourage their use as part of a joking culture. Use them against yourself as an example. This is usually not difficult, because as facilitators we often dominate, sabotage and talk too much.

13 Have you ever ...?

Ask for raised hands, or small buzz discussions, on:

Have you ever had something done to you?
What did it feel like?
and then

Have you ever done it to someone else?
In what context?

Examples are:

- Have you been put down by someone using words they know you will not know? What did it feel like? Have you done it to others? In what contexts?
- Have you had others talk in a language, without translation, that they know you do not know or cannot use fluently? What did it feel like? Have you done it to others? In what contexts?
- Have you been interrupted by someone senior to you who starts talking in the middle of your sentence forcing you to shut up? What did it feel like? Have you done it to others? In what contexts?

Option

Start with brainstorming in small groups to identify types of dominating verbal behaviour, like the above. List these. And then proceed with the questions.

14 Talkers map [see also **18**:17]

In the middle of small group discussions (on whatever topic) ask each group to identify and send out whoever has been talking most.

Give each of these talkers a sheet of paper, pen and maybe (helps but not essential) a hard surface to draw on. Ask them to return and sit inconspicuously outside their groups and draw maps showing the group members. They draw a circle round each person each time they speak. Those who speak most often end with circles enveloping others. At the end the map is shared with the group and discussed.

MAKE TALKERS OBSERVERS

Tips

- A good size of paper for the mapping is a half, third or quarter of a flip chart sheet.
- The maps can be put on the walls as a reminder.
- Remember that talkers with special knowledge, or who summarize, may be helping others.

15 Group and seat sensitively [See 11 and 12]

Dominators can be partly neutralized and the silent can be given more space in many ways through sequences of group composition and seating arrangements.

Some examples:

- Put those who talk most into the same group, similarly those who talk least. This can follow on from talkativeness ranking.
- Arrange chairs, with or without tables, with labels like 'generous talkers', 'medium talkers' 'quiet thinkers' and participants choose for themselves where to go, perhaps with a little bit of help from their friends.
- Change the membership of small group discussions.
- Send on the biggest talkers to other groups [see 11:19].
- Have plenary time after activities which leave the seating muddled up with little eye contact, and so less awareness of the size of the group.

16 Map the seating

If you notice that the choice of where to sit, or the seating arrangement, marginalizes some and empowers others, invite participants to map the seating on a flip chart. Each draws in her or his seat on the flip chart. Then buzz or discuss in plenary how the seating affects interactions.

In some contexts and cultures, I have noticed women polarize between those who sit at the back and sides, and a few who sit right in front. The map in such a case can use male and female symbols to make the point. Participants can themselves mark on a flip chart where they are sitting, using male and female symbols.

Source: Eva Robinson in Kunming, China

17 Use the ground

The democracy of the ground [see 12:18 and 14:16] reverses relationships. Uppers who stay upright are left out. Dignity disables. Lowers who get down, write and sort the cards, draw the maps, score the matrices, move the materials, take command of the process. And when uppers do get down, they dominate less: there is less eye contact, and speech loses some of its superiority; lowers can move cards, draw with chalks or change scores with stones or seeds. But be vigilant. Whose

DEMOCRATIC ON THE GROUND

reality counts may depend on who seizes a pen later in a process, as the verse suggests:

Democracy of the Ground
Watch behaviour. We detect
Dominators stay erect
If you need objective proof
See how they remain aloof
Not for them the bended knee
'Others may get down – not me!'
Playing on the lower ground
Uppers are not to be found
PRAers do much more
Freely frolicking on the floor
Maps and matrices and Venns
Made with beans and chalks, not pens
Then an end to all this caper
Time to put it all on paper
Uppers abruptly seize the pen
It's their version that's drawn then
The moral's clear for all to know
Uppers master those below
We must ever vigilant be
Ground-truthing our democracy

18 Discuss and consult

Discuss with the person concerned. Explain to the dominator that you are trying to enable those who speak little to express themselves, and to the shy and reticent that you are trying to restrain the big talkers. Ask them for their help and advice.

19 Self-scoring [see also **18**:4]

Put the numbers zero–ten on the ground or on a wall. Ask participants to reflect first on how they would score themselves on a scale for a relevant characteristic: for example, talkativeness, assertiveness, ability to listen and understand another's point of view … and then to stand there.

Encourage discussion with neighbours. Ask them then to move to where they would like to be. Then invite discussion on what they would need to do to get there.

20 Ask them

Raise the issues of silence and talking with all the participants. Ask small groups to discuss, suggest what to do and report back. This can become part of a group contract [see **5**:18].

21 Invent and improvise your own

21 Tips for Surviving Participatory Workshops

Confidential to those who are seriously shy and
have a horror of participation
For your eyes only
Solidarity please
Do not share with facilitators

Warning and Disclaimer

Read at your own risk

The author accepts no responsibility for damage to the sanity, social life, self-respect, bowel conditions or career of any person reading or putting into practice any of the advice that follows

---

This text has not been checked out with those to whom it is addressed. To have done so would have intruded on their privacy. Some actions recommended may be too extrovert. Reader, please use your own judgement. And however timid, shy or retiring you are, do please still tell me what you think. In the unlikely event of this sourcebook having a second edition, let the whisper of your voice be heard and represented.

DREAD PARTICIPATORY WORKSHOPS

You dread participatory workshops. The last thing you want is to interact (the word they use) with boisterous people who talk too much and too loud, who slap backs and may even (in some cultures) hug you. You do not want to discuss in groups or play silly games. You do not want to be facilitated to participate. You do not want to speak and face ridicule or smiles of condescension. And the ultimate nightmare: you do not want to have to role play doing something *well*, followed by public critique. And the forced hearty happiness, and all those *interactions* will be utterly exhausting. You would rather crawl into a hole. Well, take heart. Remember that *not to participate is a basic human right*.

You do not want to go. But you are sent. Someone thinks you need to become more confident, or assertive, or relaxed, or participatory, or gender-sensitive, or diversity-aware, or whatever. 'It will be good for you.' 'You will enjoy it.' '*Other people have found it helpful.*'

You cannot stand those sensitive, caring and intrusive facilitators for whom helping shy people speak is a mission. They spot you and try to 'bring you out of yourself', 'enhance your capability for self-expression', 'build your confidence', 'present you with opportunities for self-actualization' and 'nurture your growth'. Yuk!

Well, here is a survival kit. Take private pleasure as you put it into practice. Enjoy. But don't let on that you have read this, and please, never, ever, show it to one of those facilitators.

There are six strategies:

- avoid
- hide
- be insignificant
- observe and learn
- evade responsibility
- seek solace in solidarity

Avoid the Workshop

1 Escape nomination

Be alert about 'opportunities' coming up. There may be early warnings on the Internet and email if you have and use these. Arrange well in advance to have other commitments at the time. Weddings, memorial services and family holidays have varying degrees of credibility and weight. Stress their importance and the personal privacy of their details.

2 Sacrifice your place for someone else

An elegant solution. Find a colleague who would like to go or who 'truly deserves the opportunity'. Gain brownie points by giving up your place.

3 Don't go

Close to the time, have an emergency. A family crisis? Your cow has fallen down a well? The safest is to go off sick. Keep within the days off you are allowed before you need a doctor's certificate. A virus with high temperature is dodgy if anyone may come to see you. Stomach upsets are less risky but back problems are best, being common, longer lasting and easy to act.

HIDE

Hiding away during a workshop should be used with care.

4 Lie on your bed

'I don't feel very well. I'm very run down. I'll lie down for a bit. I do get this from time to time. It's nothing. I'm taking vitamin C. Don't worry about *me*. The workshop is more important. I just need to rest. I'll be all right soon. I'll come and join you as soon as I can. No, thanks, I really *don't* need a doctor…'

5 Sit in the toilet

The toilet is usually the safest and most private place (an early lesson from my National Service). But be sparing in its use. Too much absence may be noted. A caring person may seek you out and bang on the door 'Are you all right in there?' Reserve this as a fallback for critical junctures.

SIT IN THE TOILET

BE INSIGNIFICANT

Making yourself insignificant is an art form. For full aesthetic pleasure give it concentrated attention. Here are some hints:

6 Sit on a fringe

Choice of where to sit helps a lot. Those who want to participate loquaciously will sit where they can see everything and command attention. You want the opposite. Seek out seats which are variously:

- at the back;
- lower than others;
- at the edges;
- with a bad view of any board or screen (but not too close to a board);
- behind a large person with sombrero, stetson or huge hairdo;
- where hardly anyone has eye contact with you.

7 Dress drably

Choose unostentatious faded colours in brown, beige, perhaps black, but don't overdo it. Fit in with the norms, whatever they are – pullovers and jeans, suits, saris – so that you do not stand out.

8 Don't speak unless you have to

This may be no problem in a large group, but be cautious too in small groups. Be an attentive but not intrusive listener.

9 If forced to speak, mumble or stutter and look downwards

A nice balance is needed here. If you overdo it, for example, in one of those ghastly rounds where everyone has to say their name, or worse, something about themselves, or a jokey adjective to go with their name, you may actually draw attention to yourself. Someone may shout 'Speak up – we can't hear'. Listen as others speak and judge a safe level of near-inaudibility.

Any stutter should be slight. Avoid prolonged pauses which might draw attention to you as a person needing sympathy, understanding, patience and sensitive, caring help. Another problem with a stutter is keeping it up. Mumbling is safer.

MUMBLE

Another device is a verbal tick, a phrase with which you habitually pepper your sentences – 'I mean', 'to be honest', 'you see', 'well…', 'er, um' – to the point of embarrassing others. But this solution may be too extrovert for you.

10 Present the clueless self

A good opportunity is when asked your opinion. Be a little flustered, hesitate and then use one or more of these 21:

- 'This is not really my subject.'
- 'I have not yet had time to think about this.'
- 'I don't know what to think.'
- 'I would rather hear what other people have to say.'
- 'What do *you* think?'
- 'The rest of you know much more about this than I do.'
- 'I find the whole subject rather confusing.'
- 'I'm lost. Could someone clarify what xxxxxx (a jargon word) means in this context?'
- 'I'm sorry. I received the brief too late to read it.'
- 'I'm afraid I'm the last person to ask that.'
- 'I would like to know what (name a big talker) would say to that?'
- 'I find it difficult to make up my mind on this.'
- 'I'm all over the place on this.'
- 'Don't ask me' (various intonations. Practice in advance.)
- 'I was afraid you might ask me that.'
- 'I think we will make more progress as a group if someone else answers that.'
- 'I don't have a view.'

- 'I have yet to make up my mind.'
- 'I missed the introduction.'
- 'I seem to have joined the wrong group.'
- Say nothing. Look embarrassed. Blush if you can. Press your lips together, raise your eyebrows, and make a despairing gesture with your hands.

Tip

Practice the non-verbals in front of a mirror beforehand.

OBSERVE AND LEARN

11 Learn names

One big danger is the terrifying games that facilitators like for making people say each other's names. Everyone is expected to remember everyone else's name after one go, and then to demonstrate that they have done so. And of course this happens at the worst time, at the beginning of the workshop.

If you have a brilliant memory for names, this will pose no problems. But most of us do not. Leaving aside all those professional ways of learning names, here are some tips:

- Concentrate on easy names. Make sure that at least you know some.
- As people say their names, repeat them under your breath to yourself.
- Sketch a map of who is sitting where.
- List names as they are said, and use a code. One I use for men is:

S = specs
M = moustache
Be = beard
Ba = bald
P = portly

The problem is when there are a lot of the same (eg SMBaPs).

Enjoy making up your own code. Then keep learning and repeating the names to yourself. Remember, though it is cold comfort, that some others will be secretly grateful to you if you cannot remember names, because they cannot either and will be saying to themselves: 'There, but for the grace of God ...'

12 Pick out the extroverts and introverts

You need to know the extroverts in order to avoid responsibilities (see 17 below) and the introverts as allies and sources of solace (see 18 and 19 below).

EVADE RESPONSIBILITY

The most terrible fate is to have to chair a group or act as a rapporteur. Chairing a group means that you have to talk, usually, and think about the process of the group as well as what you think yourself, or think you ought to think. They will tell you it will build up your confidence, but that's the last thing you want.

Being rapporteur means that you have to listen to what others are saying, synthesize and summarize it, and then present it to the whole workshop. Others from other groups will also be presenting. You may end up with some muddled notes. Others will have well-organized overhead transparencies or flip chart sheets, together with a few well-chosen jokes. Of course, they will tell you, being a rapporteur is good for personal growth.

Avoiding these two responsibilities requires concentrated attention:

13 Choose your group with care

If participants are choosing their groups, wait until nearly all have signed up, and then pick a larger group with voluble extroverts who will want to chair and report. The gamble of going for a larger group raises the stakes but usually pays off. It makes it worse if you end up having to chair, but reduces the risk of being rapporteur.

14 Arrive late in the group

Pay a visit to the toilet on the way (if a WC, flush for credibility) and if you are noticed, mumble an apology. Alternatively, go to the wrong room so that you use up time being redirected. This way the chair and rapporteur will usually have been allocated by the time you arrive. (The risk is being 'volunteered' in your absence, especially if there is an egalitarian tyranny in which 'Everyone must have their turn'. But if you have already shown how retiring and ineffectual you are, this risk may not be high.)

15 Isolate yourself

Choose a marginal seat. It should not be central (for chair) or next to a flip chart (for rapporteur). More often than not this is self-adjusting with only marginal seats left for late arrivals. Then, crucially, when roles are being allocated, *avoid all eye contact*. Busy yourself with disorganized papers or hunt in your briefcase. Keep your head low.

16 Have a prepared excuse:

- I have to leave early (to pick up a child from school, if credible, is brilliantly unanswerable).
- I am expecting a long-distance phone call.
- I have diarrhoea.

Or if a flip chart is to be used for reporting:

- I have sprained my wrist (if a nurse or doctor in the group tries to have a helpful look laugh it off that you were just joking, which after all is more or less true).

17 Call on others

If you are trapped, propose others. This is where it helps to know the extroverts. Name them. If even this fails, your ultimate resort is to ask others to help. Simply say 'Help me!' 'How shall we proceed?' 'What would you like me to say?'. Others will usually come to the rescue.

SEEK SOLACE IN SOLIDARITY

18 Ally with others like yourself

PROPOSE OTHERS

You may prefer to keep to yourself. But there must be others who feel as you do. They may be grateful and comforted to know that they are not alone.

19 Collect and treasure incidents of awfulness

Become a connoisseur. The worse things are, the better stories they make. You may not be a storytelling type, but if you find kindred spirits, you can share experiences and support one another. Through gleeful subversion you may even begin to *enjoy*.

20 Hide these notes from facilitators

Keep them especially from anyone whose mission is to help the silent speak. Know your enemies. Keep your secrets. Make your watchword *solidarity of the shy*.

21 Invent, improvise and share your repertoire with others like yourself

If you send me details I will try to make them available to others. Oh yes, and let me know whether you prefer not to be acknowledged as the source.

21 Sources of Ideas for Trainers and Facilitators

by Robert Chambers and Jane Stevens

Sources to visit

Participation Resource Centre, Institute of Development Studies (IDS), University of Sussex

The Participation Resource Centre holds over 4000 documents, books and videos and is open 9.30am to 5.00pm Monday to Friday (as of mid-2002). Gives advice on accessing documents and other sources of information, and operates a limited information delivery service, which is currently free (2002). A database with details and abstracts of documents can be found on the Participation Group website at www.ids.ac.uk/ids/particip. Some full text documents can also be found there. Photocopying facilities are available at IDS.

For further information contact:

Participation Group, IDS, University of Sussex, Brighton BN1 9RE, UK
Tel: +44 (0)1273 678690 Fax: +44 (0)1273 621202
Email: participation@ids.ac.uk
Website: www.ids.ac.uk/ids/particip

Resource Centre, International Institute for Environment and Development (IIED)

The Resource Centre provides an information delivery service, free of charge to non-OECD countries (at cost to OECD countries). A searchable bibliographic database is available on-line. Also open to visitors by appointment for which a small charge is made.

For further information contact:

International Institute for Environment and Development, 3 Endsleigh Street, London WC1H ODD, UK
Tel: +44 (0) 20 7388 2117 Fax: +44 (0) 20 7388 2826
Email: resource.centre@iied.org
Website: www.iied.org/resource/

Resource Centres for Participatory Learning and Action Network (RCPLA)

This is an informal network of resource centres around the world committed to information sharing and networking within the framework of participatory methodologies and approaches. There are currently 15 members located in Bolivia, Egypt, India, Kenya, Mexico, Nepal, Nigeria, the Philippines, Senegal, Sri Lanka, Thailand, Uganda, the UK (x2) and Zimbabwe. Details of the members and how to contact them, along with the activities of the Network can be found on the RCPLA website at www.rcpla.org. Alternatively contact IIED as above for details of your nearest RCPLA contact. This website also provides a useful list of training, conferences and events for those interested in participation.

Websites

Many organizations have good websites offering information, resources and links on participation, facilitation, training and learning. As their details change frequently anything we list here would rapidly become out of date. However, all three websites above have links pages, kept updated, with details of other sites.

21 SOURCES TO SEND OFF FOR AND USE

These sources are chosen as places to look for ideas about what to do and how to do it. Most of them are directly relevant to convening participatory workshops. A few also cover other aspects of participation, and participatory approaches and methods. Except for the first and last, they are in reverse order of date of publication. Some more expensive sources have been excluded. Those that permit photocopying have been preferred. This is mentioned when it is explicit. Inclusion of a source here does not necessarily endorse the content. While the details of these sources are as accurate as possible at the time of going to print, they may change over time. If you have any problems with availability please get in touch with the Participation Group at IDS (details at the start of this section) and we will do our best to help you.

1

Title	*Participatory Learning and Action: A Trainer's Guide*
Authors	Jules N Pretty, Irene Guijt, Ian Scoones and John Thompson
Series	Participatory Methodology Series, Sustainable Agriculture Programme
Date	1995
Publisher	International Institute for Environment and Development, London, UK
ISBN	1 8998 2500 2
Price	£20.95
Postage	Variable

Availability   Earthprint
                      PO Box 119, Stevenage, Herts, SG1 4TP, UK
                      Tel: +44 (0)1438 748 111
                      Fax: +44 (0)1438 748 844
                      Email: orders@earthprint.com
                      Website: www.earthprint.com
                      [Also available in Spanish]

Abstract   267 pages. Though more expensive than most of these sources,
                      this is, in our view, the best. Combines how to train and facilitate
                      with a varied repertoire of exercises. Contains excellent advice on
                      training and process. Chapters in Part 1 include You, the Trainer
                      and Facilitator; Group Dynamics and Team Building; Principles of
                      Participatory Learning and Action; Training in Participatory
                      Methods in the Workshop; the Challenges of Training in the Field;
                      and Organising Workshops for Training, Orientation and
                      Exposure. Part 2 consists of 101 Games and Exercises for Trainers.
                      On piii it says 'Please feel free to photocopy what you need …
                      and distribute the information widely, if the original text is
                      properly acknowledged and the objective is not for profit or gain'.

2

Title   *Enhancing Ownership and Sustainability: A Resource Book on Participation*
Authors   IFAD, ANGOC and IIRR
Date   April 2001
Publishers   International Fund for Agricultural Development, Coalition for
                      Agrarian Reform and Rural Development and International
                      Institute of Rural Reconstruction
ISBN   1 930261 004
Price   US$15.00
Postage   Approx US$20 airmail, US$12 surface mail
Availability   Publications and Communication Program (PCP)
                      International Institute of Rural Reconstruction (IIRR)
                      Y C James Yen Center, Biga, Silang, Cavite
                      4118 Philippines
                      Tel: +63 (0)46 414 2417 (loc. 201 or 202)
                      Fax: +63 (0)46 414 2420
                      Email: Publications@iirr.org

Abstract   335 pages. A collection of short, descriptive and critical reviews of
                      participatory approaches and experiences, with sections on
                      Poverty and Participation; Participatory Processes; Participatory
                      Project Planning and Implementation; Monitoring Impact; and
                      Institutions, Partnerships and Governance. Includes (pp151–7)

'A Participatory Workshop Process to Produce User-friendly Information Materials' describing a 'writeshop' of the sort used in the development of this resource book. Copyright free. Readers are encouraged to use material extensively, with no restrictions on photocopies, lending or other uses, provided the authors and source are duly acknowledged.

3

Title	*From the Roots Up: Strengthening Organizational Capacity through Guided Self-assessment*
Authors	Peter Gubbels and Catheryn Koss
Date	2000
Publisher	World Neighbors, Oklahoma City, US
ISBN	0 942716 10 8
Price	US$20.00
Postage	Variable
Availability	World Neighbors International Headquarters
	4127 NW 122 Street
	Oklahoma City
	OK 73120, US
	Tel: +1 800 242 6387 or +1 405 752 9700
	Fax: +1 405 752 9393
	Email: actionlearning@wn.org
	Website: www.wn.org
	[Also available in French and Spanish]

Abstract   183 pages. A sourcebook for enabling grassroots NGOs and community groups to assess and strengthen their capacity. A rich source for ideas. Numerous participatory exercises are described. Chapters include guided self-assessment; preparing exercises; planning a workshop; preparing for fieldwork; working with facilitators; analysis and documentation; self-assessment; exercises for activities, performance and impact; and exercises for analysis of internal organizational issues, relationships, viability, autonomy, trends, and prioritization and action. The preplanning and strong role of the facilitator are in a VIPP and francophone West African tradition, arguably leaving scope for more handing over of the stick or pen. The format is easily photocopied. For permission to reproduce contact World Neighbors.

4

Title	*Embracing Participation in Development: Wisdom from the Field*
Editors	Meera Kaul Shah, Sarah Degnan Kambou and Barbara Monahan
Date	October 1999
Publisher	CARE, Atlanta, US
ISBN	None
Price	Free from website. Otherwise contact CARE, 151 Ellis Street, Atlanta, GA 30303, US Tel: +1 404 681 2552 Fax: +1 404 589 2624
Availability	Available free from website at: www.care.org/programs/health.reproductive_health.asp

Abstract 178 pages. Subtitled 'Worldwide experience from CARE's Reproductive Health Programs with a step-by-step field guide to participatory tools and techniques'. A first-rate up-to-date source of insights, reflections and advice focusing mainly on PLA (Participatory Learning and Action) approaches and methods. Jim Rugh's foreword is an insightful statement of issues with RRA, PRA and PLA. Part 1 (47 pages) 'CARE's experience with participatory approaches' and Part 2 (38 pages) 'Some conceptual reflections' are full of interest. Part 3 (77 pages) by Meera Kaul Shah is an excellent field guide to PLA tools and techniques, describing and illustrating 17 of these with examples and photographs, and with a section on documentation, analysis, synthesis and report-writing.

5

Title	*Participation Works! 21 Techniques of Community Participation for the 21st Century*
Authors	New Economics Foundation, with members of the UK Community Participation Network
Date	1998
Publisher	New Economics Foundation, London, UK
ISBN	1 899407 17 0
Price	£12 (organizations), £7.00 (individuals), £25.00 (bulk order of 5 copies)
Post	10% UK, 25% overseas
Availability	Central Books, 99 Wallist Road, London, E9 5LN, UK Tel: +44 (0)20 8986 5488 Fax: +44 (0)20 8533 5821 Email: mo@centralbooks.com Available in full text from the New Economics Foundation website at www.neweconomics.org/publications

Abstract   103 pages. Accessible and brief introductions to some techniques of community participation used in the UK, including Action Planning, Citizen's Juries, Future Search, Guided Visualization, Open Space, Participatory Appraisal, Participatory Theatre, Planning for Real and Social Audit.

6

Title   *Developing Technology with Farmers: A Trainer's Guide for Participatory Learning*
Authors   Laurens van Veldhuizen, Ann Waters-Bayer and Henk de Zeeuw
Date   1997
Publisher   ZED Books, London, UK in association with ETC, the Netherlands
ISBN   1 85649 490 X (paperback) 1 85649 489 6 (hardback)
Price   £12.95 (paperback), £39.95 (hardback)
Postage   £2.00 in UK, £2.50 rest of the world
Available from   ZED Books
7 Cynthia Street, London N1 9JF, UK
Tel: +44 (0)20 7837 4014
Fax: +44 (0)20 7833 3960
Email: sales@zedbooks.demon.co.uk
Website: www.zedbooks.demon.co.uk
North American distributor: Palgrave/St Martin's Press, Room 400, 175 Fifth Avenue, New York, NY 10010, US
Tel: Freephone 1 800 221 7945
Website: www.palgrave-usa.com

Abstract   A manual for trainers who train staff to work together with farmers developing appropriate technologies. It is designed to stimulate active learning. Though specific to farming, much of the content is relevant and useful for participatory training more generally, including numerous learning activities.

7

Title   *ABC of PRA*. Report on the South–South Workshop on PRA: Attitudes and Behaviour, Bangalore and Madurai, 1–10 July 1996
Editor   Somesh Kumar
Date   1996
Publisher   Institute for Participatory Practices (PRAXIS), India, and ActionAid India
ISBN   None
Price   Rs 50/-
Postage   Variable

Availability	PRAXIS – Institute for Participatory Practices
	12 Pataliputra Colony Patna – 800 013, Bihar, India
	Tel: +91 (0)612 267 558
	Fax: +91 (0)612 267 557
	Email: praxis@actionaidindia.org
	Website: www.praxisindia.org

All payments should be made by bankers cheque/demand draft drawn in the name of 'PRAXIS – Institute for Participatory Practices', payable at Patna, Bihar, India.

[Copies also available from the Institute of Development Studies – see Sources to Visit, above]

Abstract   86 pages. Reflections, insights, guidelines and exercises collected, contributed and evolved at a remarkable workshop. Includes guidelines for training sequences and processes, and tips for trainers. Can be photocopied.

8

Title	*Facilitator's Guide to Participatory Decision-Making*
Authors	Sam Kaner with Lenny Lind, Catherine Toldi, Sarah Fisk and Duane Berger
Date	1996
Publisher	New Society Publishers
ISBN	0 86571 347 2
Price	US$24.95/Can$29.95
Postage	Variable
Availability	New Society Publishers
	PO Box 189, Gabriola Island, BC, Canada, V0R 1X0
	Tel: +1 250 247 9737
	Fax: +1 250 247 7471
	Email: info@newsociety.com
	Website: webmaster@newsociety.com
	(orders can be made via website)
	In the UK available from: Jon Carpenter Publishing, Alder House, Market Street, Charlbury, Oxfordshire OX7 3PH
	Tel/Fax: +44 (0)1608 811 969

Abstract   255 pages. An excellent guide to group facilitation, with a host of insights and tips about group processes. Tips and advice cover a wide range, from how to hold several coloured marker pens to dealing with difficult dynamics. The three parts are: grounding principles; facilitator fundamentals; building sustainable agreements

Copyright   Photocopying portions of the book is encouraged for the support of group work facilitation. Photocopying to conduct fee-for-service training requires permission.

9

Title	*Training for Transformation: A Handbook for Community Workers* (Set of Books One, Two and Three)
Authors	Anne Hope and Sally Timmel
Date	1996 (first published 1984)
Publisher	ITDG Publications, London, UK (formerly published by Mambo Press, Zimbabwe)
ISBN	1 85339 353 3 (Set of Books One, Two and Three)
Price	£19.95
Postage	UK 15%, Europe 20%, rest of world standard 25%, rest of world priority 40%
Availability	ITDG Publications
	103–105 Southampton Row, London, WC1B 4HL, UK
	Tel: +44 (0)20 7436 9761
	Fax: +44 (0)20 7436 2013
	Email: orders@itpubs.org.uk
	Website: www.itdgpublishing.org.uk
Abstract	147, 131 and 182 pages. A rich source of ideas and exercises in the traditions of Paulo Freire and radical Christianity, stressing values and personal transformation. Book 1 includes the roots of the method, surveys, problem-posing and adult learning; Book 2 trust, dialogue and listening, leadership, participation, action planning and evaluation; and Book 3 social analysis to develop critical awareness.
Also	*Training for Transformation: A Handbook for Community Workers* (Book Four) (1999) ISBN 1 85339 461 0; Price £12.95. All other details as above.

10

Title	*Stepping Stones: A Training Package on HIV/AIDS Communication and Relationship Skills*
Author	Alice Welbourn
Date	1995 (first edition)
Publisher	ActionAid, London
ISBN	English: 1 87250 233 4
	French: 1 87250 245 8
Price	£20.00
Postage	Included in price
Video	Videos @ £35.00 each including airmail post/packing:
	English – available in PAL or NTSC format
	French – available in PAL , NTSC or SECAM format
	Swahili – available in PAL format only
	Luganda – available in PAL format only
	Please state which language and version (PAL, NTSC or SECAM) you require when ordering.

Availability	The manuals can be purchased as separate items, but the video cannot be bought without an accompanying manual. The full training package comprises four manuals and one video @ £115.00.
	Teaching Aids at Low-Cost (TALC)
	PO Box 49, St Albans, Hertfordshire AL1 5TX, UK
	Tel: +44 (0)1727 853 869
	Fax: +44 (0)1727 846 852
	Email: talcuk@btinternet.com
	Website: www.talcuk.org

Abstract	230 pages. The manual on its own is an inspiring source of ideas especially for participants' mutual help in workshops. Designed and presented for use in villages, it contains ideas, activities and advice of value for facilitators in all contexts.

11

Title	*Training Manual in Community Development: A Practical Guide for Trainers of Trainers and Practitioners in Community Development*
Author	ACORD Eritrea
Date	1995
Publisher	ACORD
ISBN	Mimeo
Price	Price £10.00
Postage	Included in price
Availability	ACORD
	Dean Bradley House, 52 Horseferry Road, London, SW1P 2AF, UK
	Tel: +44 (0)20 7227 8600
	Fax: +44 (0)20 7799 1868
	Website: www.acord.org.uk

Abstract	75 pages. Good ideas, exercises and material on training, especially attitudes and behaviour, listening and community development fieldwork.

12

Title	*Training Trainers for Development: Conducting a Workshop on Participatory Training Techniques*
Author	CEDPA
Date	1995
Publisher	The Centre for Development and Population Activities, Washington DC, US
ISBN	None
Price	US$15.00

Postage	US US$ 5.00, rest of the world US$15.00
Availability	The Centre for Development and Population Activities, Suite 100, 1400 Sixteenth Street NW, Washington DC 20036, US
	Website: www.cedpa.org/publications

Abstract	92 pages. A manual designed to cover basics in 12 sessions, tested in various countries. Useful as a checklist of reminders. Contrasts classroom and adult non-formal learning. The learning styles inventory looks good, and links learner roles with trainer behaviours.

13

Title	*The Guide to Effective Participation*
Author	David Wilcox
Date	1994
Publisher	Partnership Books, London, UK
ISBN	1 870298 00 4
Price	£9.95
Postage	Included in price
Availability	Partnership Books, Apt 1, 43 Bartholomew Close, London EC1A 7HN, UK
	Tel: +44 (0)20 7600 0104
	Fax: +44 (0)20 7600 0133
	Email: david@partnerships.org.uk
	Available as full text document at www.partnerships.org.uk/part
	together with a 'Guide to Development Trusts and Partnerships'

Abstract	A great deal in 65 pages. Clear, short, useful entries with ideas covering types of participation, methods, an extensive A to Z of participation and a list of useful publications.

14

Title	*VIPP: Visualisation in Participatory Programmes*
Author	Neill McKee with Hermann Tillmann, Maria Salas and others
Date	1993
Publisher	UNICEF, Dhaka, Bangladesh
ISBN	92 806 3033 4
Price	US$16.95
Postage	US$10.00 overseas

Availability   UN Bookshop
        United Nations Concourse Level
        1st Avenue and 46th Street, New York, NY 10017, US
        Tel: +1 212 963 7680
        Toll free: +1 800 553 3210 (US and Canada)
        Fax: +1 212 963 4910
        Email: bookshop@un.org
        or order via the UN website at www.un.prg/Pubs

Abstract   158 pages. A manual for facilitators and trainers involved in partic-
        ipatory group events. Includes participatory exercises and an
        ingenious range of ways of using coloured cards in participatory
        analysis on vertical surfaces. Contents include sections on VIPP
        materials and their use, planning VIPP processes, VIPP techniques,
        games and exercises, use of group and plenary, and evaluation.

15

Title   *Action Speaks Louder*
Author   A Jane Remocker and Elizabeth T Sherwood
Date   Sixth edition, 1998
Publisher   Churchill Livingstone, Edinburgh, London, Madrid, Melbourne,
        New York, Tokyo
ISBN   0 443 05865 2
Price   £22.95
Postage   £5.00 in UK, variable overseas
Availability   Harcourt Publishers Ltd
        Foots Cray High Street, Sidcup, Kent, DA14 5HP, UK
        Tel: +44 (0)20 8308 5700
        Fax: +44 (0)20 8308 5702
        Email: cservice@harcourt.com
        Website: www.harcourt-international.com

Abstract   190 pages. 26 pages of basic concepts, and then 54 exercises for
        small groups, mostly designed to enhance the capabilities and
        confidence of participants.

16

Title   *Creative Games in Groupwork*
Authors   Robin Dynes
Date   1990
Publisher   Winslow Press Limited, UK
ISBN   0 86388 078 9
Part Number 0020499

Price	£24.95
Postage	Free in UK if payment received with order, otherwise 12%. For overseas prices contact Speechmark Publishing Ltd
Availability	Speechmark Publishing Ltd
	Telford Road, Bicester OX26 4LQ, UK
	Tel: +44 (0)1869 244 644
	Fax: +44 (0)1869 320 040
	Email: info@speechmark.net

Abstract   249 pages. Included here, despite its cost and photocopying restriction, because it describes 180 games with 20 in each of these 9 sections: introduction and mixing exercises; quiet games; exuberant games; puzzles and brainteasers; verbal games; pen and paper games; quizzes; stimulating word games; and outdoor activities. No reproduction without prior written permission from the copyright holder (Robin Dynes).

17

Title	*Global Teacher, Global Learner*
Authors	Graham Pike and David Selby
Date	1988
Publisher	Hodder and Stoughton, London, Sydney, Auckland, Toronto
ISBN	0 340 402 61 X
Price	£22.00
Post	£2.50 UK, variable overseas
Availability	Bookpoint Ltd
	39 Milton Park, Abingdon, Oxon, OX14 4TD, UK
	Tel: +44 (0)1235 400 400
	Fax: +44 (0)1235 400 454
	Email: orders@bookpoint.co.uk
	Website: www.madaboutbooks.co.uk

Abstract   312 pages. Arising from the World Studies Teacher Training Project, and written for teachers in the UK, this sourcebook has much wider relevance for training and workshops as well. A wonderfully rich source of ideas and advice. Well illustrated with photographs and diagrams. In four parts: 'The Global Learner'; 'The Global Classroom'; 'The Global Curriculum'; and 'The Global Teacher'. Includes a listing of 37 practical handbooks. Pages bearing the symbol P can be photocopied without restriction.

18

Title	*Games for Social and Life Skills*
Author	Tim Bond
Date	1986
Publisher	Hutchinson Education (reprints 1990 onwards Stanley Thornes Ltd), UK
ISBN	O 7487 0339 X
Price	£14.75
Postage	£2.95 UK, variable overseas
Availability	Nelson Thornes Publishers
	Delta Place, 27 Bath Road, Cheltenham, Gloucester GL53 7TH, UK
	Tel: +44 (0)1242 228 888
	Fax: +44 (0)1242 221 914
	Email: orders@nelsonthornes.com
	Website: www.nelsonthornes.com
	10% discount for orders made on the Web

Abstract   Good practical advice on using and running games. An excellent selection of over 80 games clearly described and grouped into self-awareness, social skills, needs awareness, goal planning, planning what to do next, deciding who is important, listening, asking questions, non-verbal communication, giving and receiving feedback, barriers to communication, sharing, negotiating and compromise, trust games, relaxing and endgames.
'The user of these games is free to reproduce by any method the worksheets in association with the games but not the games themselves without infringing copyright restrictions, provided that the number of copies reproduced does not exceed the amount required in any one institution' (p6).

19

Title	*Gamesters' Handbook: 140 Games for Teachers and Group Leaders*
Authors	Donna Brandes and Howard Phillips
Date	1979
Publisher	Nelson Thornes Publishers, UK
ISBN	0 7487 0341 1
Price	£14.25
Postage	£2.95 UK, variable overseas
Availability	Nelson Thornes Publishers
	Delta Place, 27 Bath Road, Cheltenham, Gloucester GL53 7TH, UK
	Tel: +44 (0)1242 228 888
	Fax: +44 (0)1242 221 914

Email: orders@nelsonthornes.com
Website: www.nelsonthornes.com
10% discount for orders made on the Web

Abstract   140 games briefly described for social development (32), personal development (27), concentrative development (64), and introductory and warm up (17).
Also   Gamesters' Handbook Two (1982) ISBN 0 7487 0322 5; £14.25, available as above.
144 pages with 89 more games: all purpose (62), introductory (20) and group leaders (seven).

20

Title	*PLA Notes* (participatory learning and action) Nos 1–43 continuing
Author	Edited by the International Institute for Environment and Development (IIED)
Date	1988 to 2002 (continuing) (began as RRA [rapid rural appraisal] Notes)
Publisher	Sustainable Agriculture and Rural Livelihoods Programme/ Resource Centre for Participatory Learning and Action, IIED, London, UK
ISSN	1 357 938 X
Price	Free to non-OECD individuals and organizations based in non-OECD countries. Subscriptions (2002) for those from or based in OECD countries:
	Institutions: one year £75 or US$120, two years £140 or US$224
	Individuals: one year £25 or US$40, two years £45 or US$72
	Back copies are £12 each to both South and OECD (CD-ROM edition of collected back issues (1–40) also available: OECD individuals and all non-OECD £50 or US$75; OECD institutions £150 or US$225)
Postage	As above, free to the South or included in the subscription for OECD
Availability	Sustainable Agriculture and Rural Livelihoods Programme/ Resource Centre for Participatory Learning and Action, IIED, 3 Endsleigh Street, London WC1H ODD, UK
	Tel: +44 (0)20 7388 2117
	Fax: +44 (0)20 7388 2826
	Email: subscriptions@iied.org
	Website: www.iied.org/bookshop

Abstract   PLA Notes, published three times a year, is a major source for participatory methodologies. It 'enables practitioners of participatory methodologies from around the world to share their field experiences, conceptual reflections and methodological innovations. The series is informal and seeks to publish frank accounts, address issues of practical and immediate value, encourage innovation and act as a "voice from the field"'. It includes a section of tips for trainers. Most issues focus on one topic, eg 35 Community Water Management, 37 Sexual and Reproductive Health, 38 Participatory Processes in the North, 39 Popular Communications, 40 Deliberative Democracy and Citizen Involvement, 41 General Issue, 42 Children's Participation – Evaluating Effectiveness, 43 Advocacy and Citizen Participation (forthcoming), 44 Local Government and Participation (forthcoming), 45 Disability and Participation (forthcoming). Essential reading for anyone wishing to keep up to date with this rapidly evolving field. 'There is no copyright on the material and recipients are encouraged to use it freely for not-for-profit purposes only (but with full reference to the authors and *PLA Notes* series)'.

AND 21 – GO FOR IT

Title	*My Own Experiences, Inventions and Discoveries*
Author	You
Date	Whenever soon
Publisher	Typescript, email, www, photocopy, co-training, word of mouth
ISBN	Only if conventional
Price	Beyond value
Postage	Depends how they are shared
Availability	Up to you
Abstract	Potentially better than all the rest

References

[additional to those in **21** 21 Sources of Ideas for Trainers and Facilitators]

Absalom, E et al (1995) 'Sharing Our Concerns and Looking to the Future' in *PLA Notes* No 22, IIED, London, pp5–10

Attwood, H and Gaventa, J (1998) *Synthesising PRA and Case Study Materials: A Participatory Process for Developing Outlines, Concepts and Synthesis Reports,* Draft available from the Participaton Group, IDS, Brighton

Chambers, R (1997a) 'Tips for Trainers: Card Sorting on the Ground' in *PLA Notes* No 28, IIED, London

Chambers, R (1997b) *Whose Reality Counts? Putting the First Last,* Intermediate Technology Publications, London

Coover, V, C Esser, E Deacon and C Moore (1997) *Resources Manual for a Living Revolution,* New Society Publishers, Philadelphia

Fielding, W J, Riley, J with a response by R Chambers (2000) 'Preference Ranking: A Cautionary Tale from Papua New Guinea' in *PLA Notes* No 37, IIED, London

Gibson, T (1996) *The Power in Our Hands,* Jon Carpenter Publishing, Charlbury, UK

Kaim, Barbara (1997) 'Tips for Trainers: The Buses Game' in *PLA Notes* No 30, IIED, London, p84

Khan, K S (1996) *Gender Training Manual,* Shirkat Gah (Women's Resource Centre), Karachi

Lugt, J (1997) *Group Processes: An Introduction to Group Dynamics,* Mayfield Publishing Company

Maxwell, S and Bart, C (1995) 'Beyond Ranking: Exploring Relative Preferences in P/RRA' in *PLA Notes* No 22, IIED, London

New Economics Foundation, with members of the UK Community Participation Network (1998) *Participation Works: 21 Techniques of Community Participation for the 21st Century,* New Economics Foundation, London

Remocker, J and Storch, E (1992) *Action Speaks Louder: A Handbook of Structured Group Techniques,* Churchill Livingstone, London. Out of print

Shah, M K, Zambezi, R and Simasuku, M (1999) *Listening to Young Voices, Facilitating Participatory Appraisal on Reproductive Health with Adolescents,* CARE International, Lusaka and Focus on Young Adults, Washington, DC

Sellers, T (1995) *Participatory Appraisal Workshop Proceedings,* Department of Public Health Medicine, University of Hull and East Riding Health

Shaw, B and Patterson, H (1999) 'Training Tip from the PD Conference', *PLA Notes* No 36, International Institute for Environment and Development, London, pp 43–44

A Note on Equipment, Materials and Furniture

A great deal can be done, and often done better, without resorting to special materials, gimmicks or gizmos. Many of the exercises and activities in this book are feasible without much equipment or many materials. Remember that the more you use, and especially the more complex the technology, the more there is that can go wrong [see **9**:21]. However, for the technically adept and well equipped there are creative participatory ways to use overhead projectors, slide projectors, video cameras and computers. If a record is being kept of a workshop, or if collective documents are being created, computers and printers can be useful.

Many of the activities in this sourcebook involve the use of materials that can be easily manipulated, diagrammed or mapped by participants – whether on the ground, floor or wall. Some are natural objects, such as sticks, stones and seeds, and others materials that are readily available almost everywhere, such as paper, pens and chalk. These have been found to work well in urban as well as rural contexts, in widely differing cultures and in countries on every continent.

Cards are referred to in quite a number of the activities. These can be pieces of white or coloured paper, obtained in, or cut or torn into, various shapes and sizes. They can be bought or made. Half A4 is a versatile size. They can be written on, arranged and rearranged, and used for participatory listing, identifying categories, making an agenda, ranking and other forms of analysis. They can be sorted on the ground or floor, taped onto walls or fixed onto large paper sheets using tape, glue or tacks, or adhesive spray which allows repositioning. The spray works work well on a strong, light nylon fabric sheet (balloon or parachute material is good).

When using materials that need preparation that can be done on the spot, it is good to ask participants to help rather than doing it yourself.

In the spirit of this book, the key is to try things out, keep on experimenting and come up with your own favourites. There is, though, danger of becoming enslaved to things you think you need. A good participatory workshop can be held with minimal materials – but enough of them – and little or no equipment. It may often be better to concentrate on having the basics that you need (for example, pens and flip chart sheets), and enough of them, rather than spending time and effort on obtaining and using high-tech equipment. The following is NOT a list of requirements. It is simply a checklist to review:

Materials

Flip chart paper
  for direct use or tearing up for cards
Coloured marker pens
  one per participant as a rough guide
Cards
  (see above)
Wall charts
  if you use them
Masking tape
  for fixing charts, papers etc onto walls
Blank sticky labels
  for participants to write their names on
Seeds
  (large and flat are the best) as counters
Overhead projector transparencies
and pens
Coloured paper or cards
Large rolls of (butcher) paper
Coloured stickers
Post-its
Glue or gum
Blu Tack
  often leaves a mark
Nappy (diaper) pins
  for attaching charts to curtains
Drawing pins (thumbtacks)
Scissors
  for cutting cards for Venn diagramming
Stationery
Pens, pencils
Adhesive spray
  expensive but useful; 3M is one brand
Balloon material
  *(light and tough) for adhesive spray; to
  hold cards, making them moveable*
Stationery etc: pens, pencils, staplers,
elastic bands, paper clips, envelopes,
folders, pads ...

Equipment

Flip chart stand(s), boards
Overhead projector
Screen
Slide projector, slides
Video cassette(s)
Television and VCR
Extension lead
Adaptor plugs
Digital projector
Powerpoint sofware
Computer(s) and disketters
Printer(s)
Video camcorder and cassettes
Camera and films

Furniture

Chairs
  *light movable and stackable are usually
  best*
Tables
  *smallish, light and movable are usually
  best*

Subject Index

[Entries that relate to particular activities are cross-referenced giving the relevant section number in **bold**, followed by the number of the activity within that section]

Index of Named Activities

[Each entry gives the relevant section number in **bold**, followed by the number of the activity within that section]

The Community Planning Handbook

How People Can Shape Their Cities, Towns and Villages in Any Part of the World

Nick Wates

'A very clear, well-organized and extremely useful book for those who are or who ought to be promoting democratic participation in shaping the future of our communities. With its emphasis on flexibility and adaptation in the face of experience, this is a book that I will recommend to clients and colleagues alike'
J Gary Lawrence, President, **Sustainable Strategies & Solutions, Inc**, Seattle, Washington, USA

'In the global, cyberspace age, government and business need communities as much as communities need them. Nick Wates' timely book is essential reading for ordinary people and professionals who believe that the opportunities being thrown up by this new balance are there for the taking'
Mark Hepworth, Director, **The Local Futures Group**, London, UK

'This is the best practical guide to running a community planning event, and a must for community groups and councils both in the UK and abroad'
Roger Evans, Chairman, **Urban Design Group**, UK

Growing numbers of residents are getting involved with professionals in shaping their local environment, and there is now a powerful menu of tools available, from design workshops to electronic maps. *The Community Planning Handbook* is the essential starting point for all those involved – planners and local authorities, architects and other practitioners, community workers, students and local residents. It features an accessible how-to-do-it style, best practice information on effective methods, and international scope and relevance. The glossary, bibliography and contact details provide quick access to further information and support.

Pb £14.95 • ISBN 1 85383 654 0 • 232pp • Colour • Figures, boxes, index

To order, visit **www.earthscan.co.uk**
email: earthinfo@earthscan.co.uk • tel: +44 (0)1903 828 800
• fax: +44 (0)20 7278 1142

Participation of the Poor in Development Initiatives

Taking Their Rightful Place

Carolyn M Long
Institute of Development Research

'Carolyn Long's rich, historical and comparative analysis of efforts by civil society to mainstream participation in the development paradigm is an excellent and practical addition to arguments for placing the poor at the centre of development efforts'
Lisa Jordan, Program Officer, Governance and Civil Society, **Ford Foundation**, former Executive Director, Bank Information Center

'This is a superb account of the efforts undertaken by international development agencies to introduce the simple but powerful notion that the poor must participate if development is to succeed. [A]s this excellent volume makes clear, if aid agencies expect to achieve results, they will have to find ways to give a real stake to the poor'
Brian Atwood, President, **Citizens International**, former Administrator, **USAID**

'This book is a thoughtful analysis of the progress made by donors and agencies during the past decade to embrace participation as an imperative, and makes an important contribution to our understanding of how to effectively involve citizens in the donor-assisted social and economic development programmes of their governments'
Sadig Rasheed, Director, Programme Division, **UNICEF**

CAROLYN LONG is a consultant on the roles of civil society organizations in development. The INSTITUTE FOR DEVELOPMENT RESEARCH is a non-profit research and consulting organization dedicated to increasing the capacity of civil society organizations to promote just and sustainable development.

Pb £15.95 • ISBN 1 85383 761 X • 208pp • Figures, tables, index
Hb £45.00 • ISBN 1 85383 760 1

To order, visit **www.earthscan.co.uk**
email: earthinfo@earthscan.co.uk • tel: +44 (0)1903 828 800
• fax: +44 (0)20 7278 1142

Managing for Change

Leadership, Strategy and Management in Asian NGOs

Ian Smillie and John Hailey

'*Managing for Change* is the first serious comparative study of how NGOs can and do succeed in the resource-poor, often unstable and, at times, openly hostile environments of South Asia. It is a vital volume for practitioners, academics and funders interested in improving NGO performance'
Alan Fowler, author, *Striking a Balance: A Guide to Enhancing the Effectiveness of NGOs in International Development* and *The Virtuous Spiral: A Guide to Sustainability for NGOs in International Development*

'[V]ery well written... mercifully free of jargon. It is consistently clear, well structured and accessible to a non-expert. This will be a very useful guide and a valuable contribution to the literature. It will be especially useful to other NGOs who wish to emulate the achievements of ... the cases studied'
Michael Edwards, Director, Governance and Civil Society Unit, **Ford Foundation**, author, *Future Positive: International Co-operation in the 21st Century*

Managing for Change addresses the key operational issues facing NGO managers, drawing lessons from the reality of Southern NGOs. It explores areas such as the formation of strategy, effective NGO leadership, the handling of donor relations, staff motivation and development, and the management styles most appropriate to crises and change. Well written and engaging, clear and comprehensive, this is an essential sourcebook for practitioners, professional and scholars.

IAN SMILLIE is a development consultant and co-author of *Stakeholders: Government–NGO Partnerships for International Development*. JOHN HAILEY is Deputy Director of Oxford Brookes University Business School and a co-founder of the International Training and Research Centre (INTRAC).

Pb £16.95 • ISBN 1 85383 722 9 • 208pp • Tables, index
Hb £45.00 • 1 85383 721 0

To order, visit **www.earthscan.co.uk**
email: earthinfo@earthscan.co.uk • tel: +44 (0)1903 828 800
• fax: +44 (0)20 7278 1142

Creating Better Cities with Children and Youth

A Manual for Participation

David Driskell
UNESCO

Creating Better Cities with Children and Youth is a practical manual on how to conceptualize, structure and facilitate the participation of young people in the community development process. It is an important tool for urban planners, municipal officials, community development staff, non-governmental organizations, educators, youth-serving agencies, youth advocates, and others who are involved in the community development process. It offers inspiration to all who believe in the value of community education and empowerment as a fundamental building block of a vibrant and resilient civil society, and who feel concern for young people and the quality of their lives.

The manual's core ideas and methods have been field-tested in a wide range of urban settings in both developing and industrialized cities through the work of the UNESCO Growing Up in Cities project. Case studies from project sites help to demonstrate the methods in action and show how they can be customized to meet local needs. They provide lessons and insights to help ensure a successful project, and highlight the universal applicability and value of young people's participation.

The ideas and results from the country studies of the Growing Up in Cities project are presented in the companion volume *Growing Up in an Urbanising World*.

Pb £19.95 • ISBN 1 85383 853 5 • 128pp • Photographs, figures, tables, index

To order, visit **www.earthscan.co.uk**
email: earthinfo@earthscan.co.uk • tel: +44 (0)1903 828 800
• fax: +44 (0)20 7278 1142